Published by RedDoor
www.reddoorpublishing.com

ISBN 978-1-910453-34-6

A CIP catalogue record for this book is
available from the British Library

Cover design: Gemma Wilson
Design and typesetting: Gemma Wilson

Printed by Bell & Bain Ltd, Glasgow, UK

PICITURE GREDITS

pp.20, 69 Reproduced courtesy of Diageo / Diageo PLC
pp.58, 59 Reproduced courtesy of Chivas Brothers
pp.176, 178, 179, 181 Reproduced with kind permission of Kingsbarns Distillery
p.198 Reproduced with kind permission of Douglas Laing & Co.

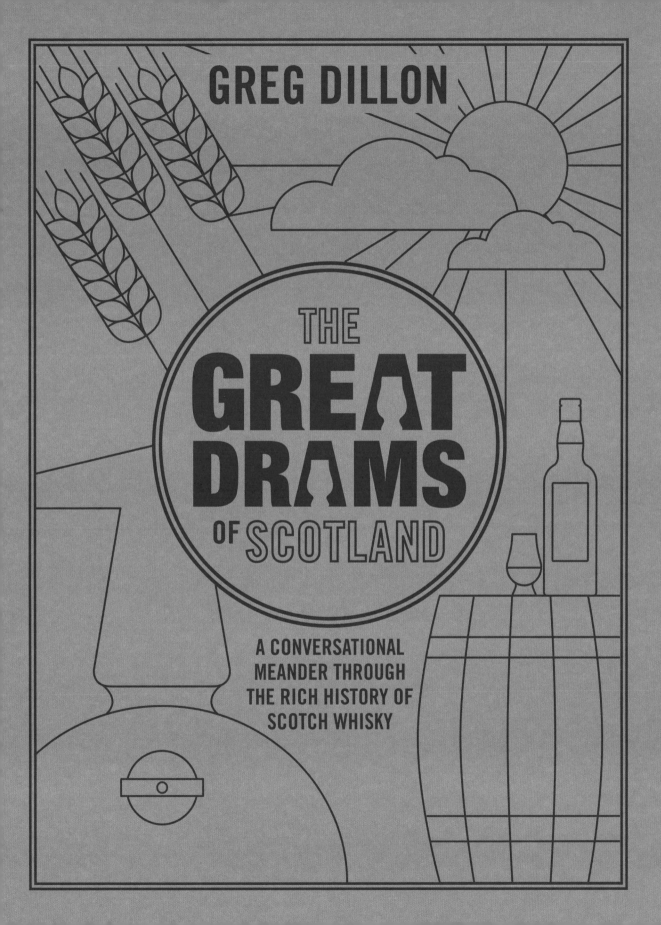

GREG DILLON

THE
GREAT
DRAMS
OF SCOTLAND

**A CONVERSATIONAL
MEANDER THROUGH
THE RICH HISTORY OF
SCOTCH WHISKY**

CONTENTS

THE PIONEERS

THE MYTHS & LEGENDS

THE CLASSICS

THE UNDISCOVERED

THE FUTURE

GREETINGS WHISKY EXPLORER

Welcome to The GreatDrams of Scotland. I'm Greg Dillon, a whisky blogger, brand consultant and writer, and I want to take you on a spirited journey through the history of the brands that have built whisky. Along the way, I will delve into what whisky is today: a drink enjoyed neat, mixed, shaken, stirred and over rocks, but above all globally loved and celebrated.

Did you realise that this has not always been the case? We will get to that in time.

My journey into whisky spans more than a decade. My late father was a whisky man. In fact, Teacher's was one of my dad's favourite whiskies. I remember seeing the bottle around the house; he would have a dram or two after a long day's work building the old family business. Years later I worked on the Teacher's brand for a few months, which was truly fascinating and the first step into doing what I do now, with William Teacher's innovative approach to the business piquing my interest in whisky.

After I began to work with more whisky clients, I suddenly thought: 'I am thinking and talking about whisky most days with clients, why am I not also blogging about it?' and thus GreatDrams.com was born.

HOW TO GET THE MOST FROM THIS BOOK

This might sound like an incredibly highbrow 'this book is too complicated' way of introducing what we are about to share, but I want you to get the most out of this book, so I'll briefly explain what you can expect…

Throughout these pages, I will be talking through the stories of a number of Scotch whisky distillery brands; a few you will have heard of, a couple may be obvious and a few form an emerging 'next generation' of whisky producers. All have their place in the world of whisky and are deserving of conversation and spotlight.

Each chapter includes a suggested whisky pairing or two. I like nothing better than sitting in a comfortable chair with a hearty measure of an appropriate whisky, and I thought you might like to get in on the act, too.

The GreatDrams of Scotland is about storytelling and bringing to life the intriguing history behind this incredible liquid, one that we can ultimately pay immense amounts of money for.

MAP OF SCOTTISH WHISKY REGIONS

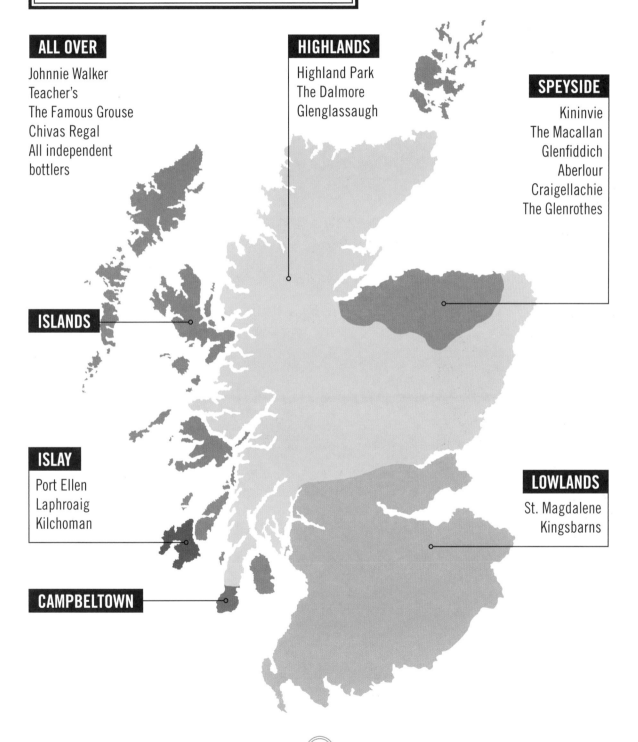

ALL OVER

Johnnie Walker
Teacher's
The Famous Grouse
Chivas Regal
All independent
bottlers

HIGHLANDS

Highland Park
The Dalmore
Glenglassaugh

SPEYSIDE

Kininvie
The Macallan
Glenfiddich
Aberlour
Craigellachie
The Glenrothes

ISLANDS

ISLAY

Port Ellen
Laphroaig
Kilchoman

LOWLANDS

St. Magdalene
Kingsbarns

CAMPBELTOWN

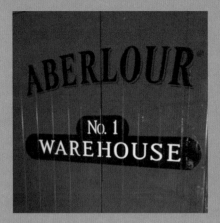

WHY BRANDING?

Well, first let me explain the notion of branding in the whisky world and where it started.

The first brand in the world was reported to be a whisky brand. Although the reality is this is hearsay and wishful thinking, the word 'brand' originates from a Norse word meaning 'to burn'. To denote the maker, a simple mark was burnt onto each whisky barrel using hot irons, before being shipped to markets around the world. This has always seemed curious, bordering on magical, to me. We are talking about the early nineteenth century here – when John Walker was a grocer, not a superbrand, Diageo was in its infancy as a one-man band, with Andrew Usher II furthering his father's attempts to perfect the art of blending whisky, and The Macallan was a small part of a farm in Speyside, not the pinnacle of luxury it is today.

Those were simpler times than today's whisky market, where NAS (whiskies with no age statement), age statements, cask finishes and a plethora of brands vie for attention.

WHAT IS A BRAND TODAY?

There are so many definitions out there. Every design agency I have ever partnered has a different, proprietary definition of what 'brand' means to them. The reality is that brand is incredibly simple to explain, yet it is bloody hard to build one that sells millions of bottles per year.

'Brand' is the visual and verbal shorthand for a product or service. More than a label or a logo, essentially it's a convincer that differentiates one product from another in otherwise crowded marketplaces. Breakfast cereal, cars or even cities…you name it, you can brand it. Even yourself. For example, my personal brand is built around my ginger beard, my bold black glasses and whisky. What's yours built around?

Brand is the expression of why people should buy into what you make versus the alternative and, when done correctly, creates a perfect harmony of product benefits that respond to subconscious consumer needs to make loyalty and purchase a no-brainer.

WHY AM I TALKING TO YOU ABOUT BRAND?

There is a lot more to a whisky brand than the taste of the liquid. This anatomy of a whisky brand explores the various elements that make up the brand, from liquid to packaging, to the personality of the people involved.

My background is in brand consulting, specifically in the whisky and luxury spirits markets where I have created, fixed and rebuilt countless brands around the world. I build my recommendations by responding to consumer needs, matching product and business competencies and expressing that through interesting storytelling.

Markets expand and contract in keeping with supply and demand. No matter how the market is moving, the winners will always be the products and services with very strong brands; they will be the ones who connect on both the rational and emotional levels that consumers require in order to make a purchase.

This is not just true of whisky. Think about Nike's 'Just Do It' positioning. It stands for exactly what it says: make things happen and be all you can be by getting on with it.

In the beer world you have Stella Artois' 'Reassuringly Expensive' message from a few years back. It stands for quality through mitigating the price point – 15–20 per cent above comparable mass lagers – and being open about quality being linked to price.

Finally, think about Glenmorangie's 'Unnecessarily Well Made' campaign, which was all about getting the message out there that whilst the average whisky drinker may not know, see or care about the process and the perfection the brand strives for, it still makes every effort because that's what makes its spirit as good as it is.

Ultimately, the whisky itself could well be the best in the world, but more often than not, the liquid itself will get you the second sale, not the first.

Allow me to explain…

Market data suggests that 42 per cent, a statistic that rises to around 63 per cent in global duty-free, of Scotch sales in the UK is accounted for by gifting purposes. Notably, much of this is chosen based on the look and feel of the bottle and secondary pack (that's the presentation tube or box that bottles often come in) as well as the stories the brand tells about the product on the front and back of the pack.

Of course, price also plays a massive role in purchasing decisions, with customers expecting to buy something within their budget, big or small, that looks and feels like a lovely gift, be it for a birthday, a colleague's leaving party or just because.

My point thus far is that whisky can be great, it can be good, it can be not so good, but it's the overarching brand experience, rather than the matured spirit itself, that we enjoy and remember the most.

THE BRAND

Whisky shoppers see the bottle in store with the associated price and stories on the label and tube. But to get to that point requires a lot of people and takes time. Here is a simplified version of what happens:

BRAND

Wants to create a product

DISTILLER

Sets the flavour profile

MARKETING

Decides on a name and briefs an agency to create the brand

Within the design agency, they set about creating something compelling for consumers.

DISCOVERY

Strategist finds out all there is to know about a brand, the competitors, the market and, crucially, the current and target consumers.

STRATEGY

Strategist, with input from the creative team, defines the strategic direction of the brand in relation to the brief and where the brand will connect best with its consumers and where it will stand out from the competition.

CREATIVE

Creative team, with input from the strategist, builds the strategic direction defined above into creative territories that give both the agency and the client options on where the packaging could go.

DELIVER

Chosen creative territory is then worked up into final designs, prototyped and built, then, once approved, produced and sent to stores.

BLOGGERS, INFLUENCERS and LAUNCH CAMPAIGNS...

...are set loose to review and engage with whisky drinkers around the world.

Blended Scotch
(Exaggerated)

CAMERONBRIDGE – GRAIN – 60%
MALTS – EACH A SMALL %

Auchroisk • Benrinnes
Blair Athol • Caol Ila • Cardhu
Clynelish • Cragganmore
Dailuaine • Dalwhinnie •Dufftown
Glendullan • Glen Elgin
Glenkinchie • Glenlossie • Glen Ord
Glen Spey • Inchgower • Knockando
Lagavulin • Linkwood • Lochnagar
Mannochmore • Mortlach • Roseisle
Strathmill • Talisker • Teaninich

SINGLE MALT
(Exaggerated)

Highland Park 12 Sherry Cask
Highland Park 12 Bourbon Cask
Highland Park 12.5
Highland Park 16
Highland Park 16.5
Highland Park 15.5
Highland Park 12.25
Highland Park 17
Highland Park 19

SINGLE CASK

Ardbeg 8 Year Old
Sherry Cask Matured
filled April 2008,
bottled April 2016,
Cask number xxxx

CHAPTER ONE

SOME SWIFT DEMYSTIFICATION

Suggested whisky:

your day-to-day favourite

(This chapter will only take a few minutes of your time)

SINGLE MALTS ARE BETTER THAN BLENDS

The perception amongst many whisky drinkers and commentators is that single malts are best. This is patently untrue. Anything other than single cask Scotch is a blend. Let that settle.

Single malt Scotch whisky is still a blend, but it is a blend of whiskies from one distillery, whereas blended Scotch whisky is a blend of whiskies from multiple distilleries.

According to many sources across the industry, blends make up over 90 per cent of the global whisky market. Seriously. They are enjoyed the world over by whisky newbies through to whisky connoisseurs and collectors, and it's all because they came first, commercially at least. Single malt as we know it only started being sold to consumers in 1963 (more on which whisky brand launched the first single malt later), but prior to that, single malt was reserved for the lucky distillery workers and locals. Everyone else was interested in blends, or so they thought.

I always think of single malt as being the perfect expression of a distillery's product, whereas I view blends as being a blender's masterpiece. The skill of the blender is in crafting the same flavour profiles year after year, batch after batch, bottle after bottle, not to mention using whiskies made with different ingredients than were available the previous year.

WHISKY IS MATURED IN SCOTLAND FOR A MINIMUM OF THREE YEARS, AS THAT'S WHEN THE SPIRIT IS DEEMED GOOD ENOUGH TO BE CALLED WHISKY

No, this is not really the case. It is, as with so many things in life, the result of a bit of 'give and take' in a taxation negotiation.

Let's delve a bit deeper…

The requirement to mature whisky for at least three years was not passed into law until the Immature Spirits (Restriction) Act of 1915, yet, as we know, whisky itself has been around for two or three hundred years. However, whisky in the eighteenth century was largely referred to as 'fresh from the still' as it was effectively 'new make', the clear concentrated spirit that runs from the still and is filled into casks to mature into whisky, or very young spirit.

The Act was brought in to pacify the then Chancellor of the Exchequer, Lloyd George, a passionate anti-boozer who felt that the ills of alcohol were damaging the United Kingdom during the First World War almost as much as the enemies they were fighting at the time. He did have a point: there is credible evidence to suggest that young, unmeasured spirit caused a lot of damage to individuals' bodies to the extent of making them blind and unfit – hence the term 'blind drunk' – to help in the war effort. Lloyd George proposed an outright ban on alcohol during the war, a prohibition of sorts, but that was met with the obvious outcry you'd expect from a nation partial to a tipple or two.

Then in stepped a chap called James Stevenson, a whisky man who went on to become the chairman of Johnnie Walker but who at the time served the war effort by overseeing the Ministry of Munitions. He pointed out that without alcohol production during the war, there would be no alcohol available to make

high explosives or anaesthetic, amongst other things. A deal was struck. The man had a point.

In one simple twist of legislative fate whisky went from being a menace to the British society of the time to a thought-through, planned and quality product.

So essentially, if you boil it down, the three-year minimum maturation period for whisky was enacted to slow supply in order that the government could stop drunken folk handling munitions during the First World War.

Whilst the romance of 'bottled when ready' is lovely, the reality is a lot more practical and rooted in political tussles.

THE OLDER AND HIGHER PRICED THE WHISKY, THE BETTER IT IS

Again untrue. Whisky tasting notes are incredibly subjective; we all enjoy whisky in different ways and are able to pick out different flavour compounds. Put it this way: if we all got the same thing from each whisky, we'd only need one whisky brand. We might all either love or hate peated whisky, for example, or prefer first-fill sherry-matured whisky to first-fill bourbon-matured whisky, but wouldn't that be dull?

Older whiskies naturally command a price premium, but in all honesty they are not always the best whiskies on the planet; price is a quality and rarity signifier more than an indicator of taste.

I have been fortunate enough to try many whiskies – the rough count is in the mid-four figures as it stands – and I have one anecdote that captures my view on the perfect age of whisky.

Myself and several other whisky writers were invited to a blind tasting of six single-cask whiskies by The Scotch Malt Whisky Society (SMWS) a couple of years back. We all went through the evening at the same pace, drinking the samples in the same order, no variables whatsoever. Two whiskies were in their thirties, two were in their twenties, two were sub-ten years old, but we didn't know that at the time. At the end of the evening we all had to submit our favourites, and a single-cask whisky aged nine years won the bulk of the votes. Humbling and a welcome reminder for all involved that age is but a number; it is how you enjoy the whisky that matters.

Older whiskies naturally command a price premium, but in all honesty they are not always the best whiskies on the planet

One other point is that I have been able to try three fifty-year-old whiskies: two were sublime; the other was probably one of only two whiskies ever I have not enjoyed. Age is not always an indicator of quality.

Now a curveball: some of my favourite whiskies are NAS (see page 23 for explanation), and happily in the sub-£50 price bracket. Whiskies such as Talisker Storm, Rock Oyster, Big Peat, The Famous Grouse Smoky Black and many more are absolutely superb and will not break the bank whatsoever.

ALL WHISKY IS GOOD WHISKY

Sadly not. The cask the spirit goes into makes up around 70 per cent of the flavour of the end whisky, but this figure varies depending on who you speak to.

The now-ex-Master Blender for The Famous Grouse, Gordon Motion, once told me:

'You can put great spirit in poor casks and you will get a reasonable whisky, but you put a good spirit in incredible wood and you have something astounding.'

So there you have it: good whisky takes time, pure ingredients and a whole load of nurturing. There are no shortcuts and there are reasons some are more highly thought of than others.

'You can put great spirit in poor casks and you will get a reasonable whisky, but you put a good spirit in incredible wood and you have something astounding'
– Gordon Motion

DIAGEO ARE EVIL

This could not be further from the truth. Without multinational Diageo, the Scotch whisky industry that we know and love today would be very different, almost unrecognisable. Its vision to create stockpiles of amazing whisky, its ownership of more than twenty distilleries in Scotland, and the fact that the company owns the mammoth Johnnie Walker brand should be testament to how fundamental it is to Scotch whisky. Not to mention the brands it owns in other drink categories.

#NOTANAD, I'm not being paid to say this. Diageo gets a bad rep for its dominance but many whisky brands simply wouldn't exist without it and the market would be a lot more fragmented. Would we have a global powerhouse such as Johnnie Walker adorning Formula One Grand Prix stands, or the low-cost entry-level blends (and other spirits) in pub chains the world over, or even the lobbying power to change legislation and move the industry on? I think not.

More importantly, Diageo plays a huge part in our enjoyment of various blends and single malts.

WHISKY IS A MAN'S DRINK

That's just bullshit. Whisky is anyone's drink provided you are over the legal drinking age in your country of residence. Whisky drinkers have evolved at a faster rate in the last ten years than in the previous century; no longer is the typical dram sipper a forty-five-plus male sat in an 'old man's pub' drinking volumes of bitter being bitter about the world and muttering between measures of their finest whatever-is-the-cheapest whisky.

No matter your sex, your age, your profession, your race, your whatever: whisky is for you

The whisky drinker of today varies around the world, but they all have a few things in common:

They are younger than a decade ago. New Asian whisky drinkers average around the twenty-eight-year-old mark whereas single malt drinkers in more developed markets average between twenty-eight and thirty-two years old.

Whisky drinkers are no longer mostly blokes. New-to-whisky drinkers are a lot more evenly split between men and women, especially in developing markets where around 40 per cent are women. In mature markets such as the UK, women account for over 30 per cent of whisky drinkers.

These people stand for individuality and exploration. It doesn't matter if you are a man or a woman when it comes to whisky – why should you be pigeonholed? The whisky drinkers of today are not predictable stereotypes; they want what they want on their terms, not that of the brands or their peers.

CHAPTER TWO

DEFINITIONS

Suggested whisky:

Another dram of your day-to-day favourite

Whisky can be a tough drink and subject to master; there are so many different terms alien to other product categories. So to help you through this book, and in your whisky exploration, here is a run-through of some of the key terms.

Now, this will not be an ABC of whisky. I think it makes more sense to explain one key whisky term up front then to guide you through how to read the detail on a whisky label.

THE ONE KEY TERM TO FIRST UNDERSTAND

NAS – No Age Statement

Simply put, NAS is a bottle of whisky without a number on it. For example:

- Age statement: Laphroaig 10
- NAS: Ardbeg Alligator

This is a big one, and referred to a few times within these pages. For those unfamiliar with this, the NAS whisky debate centres around the increasing presence of No Age Statement whisky.

A large part of the whisky world believes the best whisky has a number on the bottle, whereas there's a growing rationale that says age is just a number and that a liquor should be judged on taste rather than age.

I'm in the camp of the latter.

Whilst I would never say no to a The Macallan 30 Year Old or Glen Grant 50 Year Old or Highland Park 40 Year Old, I do appreciate that the number can be a real red herring.

My view is simple: NAS whisky provides producers with a chance to continue their phenomenal global growth.

With age-communicated whiskies, you have a bottle that contains a plethora of casks, the youngest of which has been aged the amount of time denoted on the bottle, right? With NAS whiskies you have something different. You have the ability for Master Blenders and Master Distillers to experiment, to play, to create, to ask 'What if?' – to craft something truly special and to define their time at the helm.

NAS whisky has been driven forward by the surge in the global whisky demand, which has depleted aged stock. Quite simply, distillers and brands twenty or thirty years ago did not think the market would boom the way it has. Why would they? As such, distillers did not lay down the volume of stock required for a sudden and sustained spike in global demand.

Nowadays, distillers and blenders are a lot freer to craft these unique liquids in the way I mentioned and, in my humble opinion, this can only be a good thing for both market and consumer. We see new expressions and experiments coming to fruition, from cask finishes to more diverse strains of barley, to peat levels, to all manner of different variables that are now showing up in bottles of our favourite liquor.

To summarise: I think NAS whisky is a great thing, one that can only benefit our long-term enjoyment and exploration of this great spirit.

READING THE DETAIL ON A WHISKY LABEL

Generally speaking, but not always, there are nine details to note on any whisky label you come across:

PRODUCED AND BOTTLED IN SCOTLAND

EST. YEAR (i.e. the year the distillery was established) — Est. 1899

DISTILLERY NAME (brand) — *The* DISTILLERY

REGION — HIGHLAND MALT SCOTCH WHISKY

AGE (not always present) — AGED {12} YEARS

TYPE OF WHISKY (i.e. single malt, blended Scotch, single cask) — SINGLE MALT

TYPE OF WOOD AGED/FINISHED IN — SHERRY CASK FINISHED

BOTTLE SIZE

STRENGTH, KNOWN AS ABV (alcohol by volume) — 50% ALC. BY VOL.

PPM (phenol parts per million) — PPM: 20

75CL

Along with these 'standard' details, be prepared to find the occasional addition such as:

- Collection (e.g. Glenfiddich's Age of Discovery collection)
- Bottler (e.g. Douglas Laing & Co)
- Master Blender
- Master Distiller
- Cask number
- Non-chill filtered
- The words 'Limited Edition'
- The words 'Single Cask'

It's a lot to take in, but what do they all mean? The following explanations will help. By the end you will know exactly how to read a whisky label.

Distillery name (brand)

Simple one this: the distillery name is more often than not also the brand name. Exceptions occur when distilleries sell their product on to blenders or bottlers, who then buy casks to finish or blend to create unique products released under their own name.

Type of wood aged/finished in

All whisky must be aged in oak for a minimum of three years. Bourbon, with a shorter minimum ageing period, has to be aged in new casks whereas Scotch can be aged in new or used casks, which means that often you will see 'Matured in a Sherry Butt' or 'Refill Bourbon Cask' on the label to give an indication of the taste cues you will experience.

Ex-sherry casks will add sweetness to the whisky, whereas ex-bourbon casks add an increased depth of flavour. Innovation trends are leading to some brands 'finishing' various whiskies in different types of wood, such as ex-port, ex-cognac and, more recently, ex-cider casks.

Age

Another easy one: the age of the youngest liquid in the bottle. Scotch whisky law dictates that a spirit is not considered whisky unless it has been in an oak cask for a minimum of three years. Single malts and blends facilitate easy navigation through the tiers of their products using clear age delineations.

Scotch whisky law dictates that a spirit is not considered whisky unless it has been in an oak cask for a minimum of three years

Importantly, although the age on the label refers to the youngest whisky in the bottle, there are more often than not samples from much older whiskies in each bottle, which create the complex flavours we all get to enjoy. Remember though, whisky only ages in oak, not the bottle, so once bought it does not get older in maturation terms if left in the bottle for years.

OTHER WHISKY/WHISKEY PRODUCING COUNTRIES

ICELAND

CANADA

AMERICA

Region/Type of Whisky

There are many countries where whisky (or whiskey) is produced. Scotland is the spiritual home of whisky, with five distinct whisky-producing regions: Campbeltown, Lowlands, Highlands (including Islands), Speyside and Islay.

Each has its own characteristics and flavour profiles, and it's well worth trying them all if you can to see what your palate prefers.

Strength, known as ABV (alcohol by volume)

ABV is always expressed as a percentage. The percentage relates to the ration of ethanol to water in the liquid at 20°C. So an ABV of 53% means that 53% of the liquid is ethanol and 47% is water, although within the spirit there are also 'congeners' which are by-products of distillation that form the flavour compounds that give a distillery's spirit its specific character.

Typically unaged spirit comes off the stills at around 70–75% ABV but this stuff is not consumed by the public, for relatively

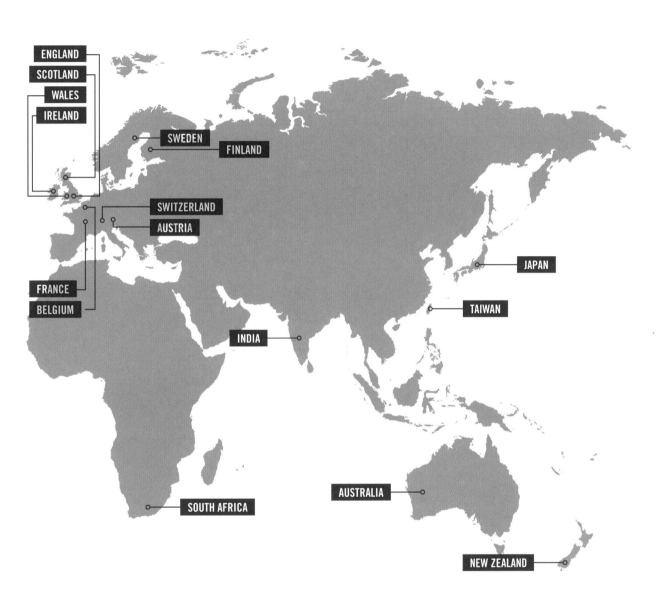

ENGLAND
SCOTLAND
WALES
IRELAND
SWEDEN
FINLAND
SWITZERLAND
AUSTRIA
JAPAN
TAIWAN
FRANCE
BELGIUM
INDIA
SOUTH AFRICA
AUSTRALIA
NEW ZEALAND

obvious reasons. As the spirit moves towards the maturation stage the ABV is typically brought down to 40% using distilled water, with many releases you will be used to seeing in stores clocking in between 40% and 46% ABV, although 'cask strength' releases can be anywhere from 50% to upwards of 61% ABV depending on age, filling strength (which is normally 63.5% ABV) and where it is matured. For example, hotter countries have a strange reversal of alcohol and water balance as the spirit matures so the ABV actually rises through maturation as water evaporates instead of the ethanol. That's the magic of distilling for you.

PPM (phenol parts per million)

This is one of the ways in which distilleries can give their whisky a unique character. To put it crudely, PPM is a measure of 'peatiness' in whisky. The phenols come from the smoke of a peat fire and are absorbed by the malt whilst it is drying, leading to different levels of peatiness depending on the length of time the smoking takes place.

Bottle size

In the UK the standard bottle size is 700ml (70cl), as per EU directives of 1992, whereas in the US the standard size is 750ml (75cl). As an aside, miniatures are typically 50ml and in travel retail stores, i.e. duty-free, the standard bottle size is 1 litre.

Collection (e.g. Glenfiddich's Age of Discovery collection)

Whisky brands are increasingly releasing collections of whisky products, for the collectability of associated products as well as to take consumers on a journey of the senses within their specific portfolios.

Examples include Johnnie Walker's Explorer's Club Collection, Glenfiddich's Age of Discovery collection, The Dalmore's Constellation Collection and Glenfiddich's Cask Collection.

PPM VALUES

Here are some examples of the PPM values of some well-known distilleries (the approximate PPM of their malt is in brackets in increasing value)

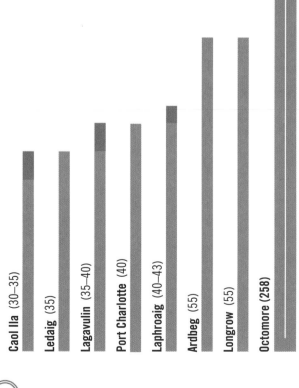

Bunnahabhain (1–2)
Bruichladdich (3–4)
Springbank (7–8)
Benromach (8)
Ardmore (10–15)
Highland Park (20)
Bowmore (20–25)
Talisker (25–30)
Caol Ila (30–35)
Ledaig (35)
Lagavulin (35–40)
Port Charlotte (40)
Laphroaig (40–43)
Ardbeg (55)
Longrow (55)
Octomore (258)

Bottler (e.g. Douglas Laing & Co)

Often, distilleries sell excess stock to independent bottlers who subsequently release their own products, so the label may indicate that this cask was selected by the company that bottled this whisky, and therefore they are most likely not the owners of the distillery. We will explore this in more detail later on.

Master Blender/Master Distiller

Obvious one really, this is the person ultimately responsible for the creation of the liquid, the taste and overall quality of what you are about to sip. The more premium the whisky, the more likely it is that the signature will become more prominent and/or handwritten as a public sign of accountability.

Cask number

The number of the cask that the whisky was bottled from, otherwise referred to as batch number if it's a specific release/edition.

Non-chill filtered

When whisky has ice or water added, it can naturally go cloudy due to the temperature decrease. Some consumers, brands and distilleries perceive this cloudiness to lead to a negative consumption experience, so instead, before bottling, some producers opt to chill the whisky down and filter out the elements that create cloudiness. Hence, non-chill filtered or 'natural' whisky tastes have become a way of distinguishing between liquid types, experiences and perceived quality in the whisky world and are often called out on pack. This is reserved for certain releases, typically mass-market blends, or entry level single malts, and worth noting that some minor filtration takes place for every whisky release to remove the little impurities and remnant cask char that makes it way into the liquid itself.

The words 'Limited Edition'

There are loads of limited-edition whiskies on the market, normally created to mark the launch of new permanent expressions with limited stock availability. These are highly collectable and often seen as trophies of whisky collections.

The words 'Single Cask'

Single cask (also known as single barrel) whiskies are bottled from an individual cask, and often the bottles are labelled with specific barrel and bottle numbers.

Now that's over with, let's crack on

THE PIONEERS

CHAPTER THREE

JOHNNIE WALKER

Suggested whisky:

Johnnie Walker Double Black
(or Johnnie Walker Platinum Label)

Johnnie Walker is the best-selling blended Scotch whisky worldwide, shipping 17.9 million cases in 2014 (The Spirits Business), which is around three or four times more than its global competitors Grant's and Ballantine's.

Be under no illusion, this is a mega brand and one built nearly entirely on lifestyle. Sure, there was a John Walker, and he was a grocer back in the day, but today John Walker's whisky label is present in around 200 countries as the world's best-selling whisky.

The Johnnie Walker journey starts in 1820, when John Walker decided he wanted to use the Walker family's grocery shop to take the inconsistent single malts being sold in and around Kilmarnock and blend them together to see if he could create a better quality product. His creations caused quite a stir and the blending business took off at a time when large-scale distilling was becoming reliable and a lot less volatile.

Alexander Walker took over the business when he inherited it in 1857. After spending a couple of years getting to grips with the emerging world of whisky, Alexander began his quest to turn the Johnnie Walker product into a global brand.

Whilst the product still bears the name of John Walker, it was to Alexander we owe a lot as it was he that started using the square bottle that was the forefather to today's iconic bottle

Whilst the product still bears the name of John Walker, it was to Alexander we owe a lot as it was he that started using the square bottle that was the forefather to today's iconic bottle structure

structure. He also came up with the idea of the slanted label, which went against category codes of the time when everything was straight, clinical and devoid of standout.

The third distilling generation of the Walker family, Alexander's sons Alexander II and George, were responsible for expanding the range to cater for more whisky flavour preferences with the addition of Red Label and Black Label. This pair of Walkers was also credited with one of the first-ever alcohol-related consumer advertising campaigns: they marketed their Johnnie Walker product to drinkers instead of the standard trade advertising expected of

them in 1906 that was functional, long-form and largely uninspiring.

KEEP WALKING

Have you ever stopped and wondered about the origins of the Striding Man who traverses more than a hundred million bottles of whisky produced every year?

Created by a chap named Tom Browne in 1908, the Striding Man has been a permanent fixture on every Johnnie Walker bottle since the 1930s. Browne was approached to design

Left: The Johnnie Walker Brand Home at the Cardhu Distillery, Scotland.

Above: The beautiful scenery surrounding the Cardhu Distillery.

the iconic symbol following an unsuccessful competiton that asked entrants to devise a way of bringing Alexander Walker II's grandfather's spirit to life.

The brand is a celebration of what's possible. The iconic tagline, 'Keep Walking', has, for many years, resonated with consumers around the world on different levels, all the time linking to personal progress. From inspiring people to keep their heads up during various conflicts around the world, to moving the civil rights movement forward, to giving whisky drinkers in various countries the motivation to be all they can be, Johnnie Walker is the label of choice.

This was not a Johnnie Walker campaign as such, but a way of being for the brand; its consumer base, and ideally the wider world, would be inspired by the Striding Man. The 'Keep Walking' message resonated with not one but a set of several generations looking for progress and betterment of self and society.

By imbuing a sense of meaning in the Striding Man, and with the positivity around the 'Keep Walking' tagline, Johnnie Walker transcended the rational 'buying a bottle of whisky' motives and elevated the brand into something that linked a product to a global set of personal values.

In an effort to continue to reach the ever-evolving whisky drinker, the dominant Millennials and the emerging Generation Y consumer (aged between twenty-five and thirty-five years old), the folks behind Johnnie

Walker furthered the 'Keep Walking' message by introducing 'Joy Will Take You Further'. According to Ivan Menezes, CEO of Diageo, during the 2015 launch, the campaign would help the brand reach a new 'golden age of Scotch'.

The premise is relatively simple: you will only truly progress if you experience joy by living for the moment. With this extension to the message, Johnnie Walker continues to transcend boundaries, borders and demographics to inspire the next generation or the few who want to be all they can be. Whilst this 'living life' or carpe diem message is not a new idea, the power of Johnnie Walker to reinvent its brand in keeping with how the consumer is evolving is fascinating.

But what of the whiskies? Why are they loved and why do their bottles sell at a factor of three to their nearest competitors?

They are very smooth, inoffensive, flavoursome and have enough levels in the range to give an accessible premium in markets the world over. The emerging global middle class in areas such as China, the US and South America are looking to show their wealth earlier in life, looking to stand out from the masses and to enjoy life more publicly than previous generations maybe did. Johnnie Walker can be the facilitator and catalyst for these aspirations.

Its range comprises six main expressions as well as limited-edition whiskies and packaging designs from time to time; Johnnie Walker has quite a comprehensive line-up of whiskies to suit every palate.

Above left: Johnnie Walker's well deserved Royal Warrant, present on each of the bottles the brand sells to their millions of loyal consumers around the world.

Above right: The iconic home of Johnnie Walker at the Cardhu Distillery, Scotland.

Why I chose this chapter's suggested whisky

I have called out Johnnie Walker Double Black and Johnnie Walker Platinum as the suggested whiskies for this chapter. Platinum's smooth palate, depth and design really impressed me a couple of years back when I first bought a bottle upon its launch. Double Black, meanwhile, is a good value dram with a really strong Islay backbone to it.

Really worth picking these up, neither release will break the bank and they are good premium Johnnie Walker options to keep in the house for when you fancy one or a few drams.

CHAPTER FOUR

TEACHER'S

Suggested whisky:

The Ardmore Legacy

'Teacher's?!' I hear you cry. Yes Teacher's, the whisky which professes to be Highland Cream, despite no one really knowing what that means. Sounds a bit like a Bailey's alternative if you ask me…

Despite not being fashionable and always on offer, I have a surprising amount of love for Teacher's Blended Scotch Whisky, more at any rate than I think many of my peers would profess, as it was the first whisky brand I worked on and it is built on innovation and intrigue as much as the liquid itself.

Did you know, for example, that William Teacher was a man ahead of his time? Originally a grocer, not only did he open the UK's first non-smoking bar, known as a 'dram shop', but he also invented the mechanism that would inspire the ration card used by the British Government during the Second World War.

It was in Teacher's dram shops, opened in 1856, that William wanted his blends to sing, to be understood and to be enjoyed. Patrons, most notably sailors on shore leave, were quite literally banned from being inebriated and from smoking, a good century and a half ahead of smoking being banned in England.

Had you entered his dram shop, you'd have been expected to abide by these rules:

- No smoking
- No round buying
- No getting drunk

Imagine if a bar had these same rules nowadays.

It was in Teacher's dram shops, opened in 1856, that William wanted his blends to sing, to be understood and to be enjoyed

So why did people continue to frequent and, in turn, make these dram shops a roaring success? Simple: most public houses were known to sell dodgy booze, often straight from the still or distilled using untoward techniques. William Teacher cornered the market for a premium blended Scotch available in sensible measures; he was a quality blender with a strong ethos.

You have to remember too that he was serving at a time when lots of workers were paid their wages in pubs, meaning much of their earnings were spent nigh on immediately on alcohol. Spirits, and whisky in particular, were a really compelling 'release' from the hell of real life back then. Sadly, it is no exaggeration to say that people were paid sod all, worked in awful

conditions and in many cases would rather be blind drunk than face the reality of their day-to-day lives.

In the UK, Teacher's has a somewhat unfortunate reputation owing to years of being beaten down on price by supermarkets. This is mainly due to Christmas and Easter loss-leading discounts. The perception of Teacher's around the world is a very different story.

In India, Teacher's ranks in the upper echelons of the whisky world and has a status that attracts business folk and younger audiences alike. The spirit is even classed as a local whisky as it is shipped over there in large tankers, which are then bottled locally. In South America, Teacher's has a reputation for being a

In India, Teacher's ranks in the upper echelons of the whisky world and has a status that attracts business folk and younger audiences alike

fun whisky for mixing and enjoying on the beach with friends, and across the globe it is celebrated as being accessible, interesting and fun.

The Ardmore is the core malt component in the Teacher's blend, and as such, understanding this whisky is crucial to understanding the Teacher's blend. Based alongside a railway line up in Aberdeenshire, Ardmore is a really quaint distillery and, now I think of it, the first Scottish distillery I visited. It is operated by a faithful crew of interesting people that care so much about their end product that you cannot help but admire them.

You don't see older bottles around a lot but if you do then it's well worth picking one up. Try independent bottlers such as the Scotch Malt Whisky Society too, as the spirit they produce there is lovely and it will give you a better appreciation for the Teacher's blend as a whole. However, The Ardmore is just one of thirty single malts and grain whiskies that make up Teacher's Blended Scotch whisky. A high percentage of the blend is single malt which helps to create that smooth, full flavour.

Left: The beautiful copper stills at Ardmore Distillery.

Right: Some fabulous Ardmore spirit resting until it is time to be sent away for blending into Teacher's Blended Scotch.

Right: There's a lot of maturing magic behind these big red doors…

Below: Barrels awaiting filling at the Ardmore Distillery.

Teacher's was the first whisky that taught me the power of the Master Blender and what they do; the art of blending is maintaining a consistent flavour without retaining consistent ingredients, and the innovation the brand stood for should be an inspiration to all whisky brands today and tomorrow. Where Glenfiddich, as you will discover later in this book, was the first single malt brand to ship 1,000,000 cases, Teacher's was selling a million cases in the UK alone as far back as 1972.

So next time you see Teacher's, or indeed The Ardmore, in a supermarket or specialist store, you'll know that there is far more depth to the brand and the liquid than the price would suggest.

Why I chose this chapter's suggested whisky

The Ardmore Legacy is a relatively new NAS Ardmore expression to the market, released just a couple of years ago. I love how the peaty notes sing whilst the liquid is calm and highly sippable. In my many whisky tastings it always surprises me how newcomers to Scotch love these notes, even when they're not expecting it.

CHAPTER FIVE

THE FAMOUS GROUSE

Suggested whisky:

The Famous Grouse 16 Year Old

Unlike a lot of the blended Scotches at the time, The Famous Grouse was not named after its blender or founder, Matthew Gloag. Instead, Gloag opted to name his product after Scotland's national game bird, the red grouse.

The brand dates back to 1896 and, in a similar vein to John Walker and William Teacher, its founder began as a merchant. Gloag, far from being a basic grocer, however, was a wine and spirits merchant from Perth and it was his daughter, Philippa, who designed the very first label for The Famous Grouse brand. Examples of the original artwork can be found at The Glenturret distillery in Crieff where the primary malt content for The Famous Grouse is produced.

Gloag was a perfectionist and believed in quality to the nth degree, something that he passed on to future generations, with William Gloag, his son, stating in 1868:

> *'It is of paramount importance that the very best materials that can be procured should be used in the manufacture of whisky.'*

It is a tradition that continues today.

The reality is that the product is very good; The Famous Grouse Smoky Black especially is a superb whisky for both quality and enjoyment

Similar to Teacher's, The Famous Grouse gets a bit of a bad rep in that it has been beaten down on price and perception by supermarkets over the years. The reality is that the product is very good; The Famous Grouse Smoky Black especially is a superb whisky for both quality and enjoyment.

What is also interesting about the Gloag whisky philosophy is that he supposedly referred to the use of sherry casks in the whisky ageing process as being of an 'unpurchasable benefit' to whisky production. Admirable really when you think about the cost of sherry casks compared to the much cheaper bourbon casks nowadays.

Above: An example of some old school The Famous Grouse packaging.

Right: Casks outside The Glenturret Distillery.

Far right: A beautiful stained glass grouse at The Famous Grouse brand home; The Glenturret Distillery.

Nowadays, The Famous Grouse ships over 37 million bottles of its core product per year, as of 2015. Until recently it was looked after by Master Blender Gordon Motion, who is not only a thoroughly lovely bloke but also incredibly passionate and detail-oriented by his very nature.

Gordon trained as Master Blender Designate for two years before ascending to the position of main man in 2009. Until early 2016, when he passed the baton on to Kirsteen Campbell, who also holds the title of Master Blender of the Cutty Sark brand, he carried on the tradition of 'good wood', telling me back in 2015:

'The wood is of the utmost importance; you can put good spirit into a poor cask and it will always make a poor whisky, but putting poor spirit into a good cask will inevitably create a good whisky. The wood is incredibly important, hence why today [in 2015] American bourbon casks cost about £100 whereas American and European sherry casks cost around €1,000.'

Wood aside, part of the malt component in The Famous Grouse is produced at the aforementioned oldest working distillery in Scotland, The Glenturret. Lucy Whitehall, The Famous Grouse Global Brand Ambassador, told me: 'We call Glenturret the heart malt, as although it's a small volume malt component in the blend, it only contributes to the blend of The Famous Grouse and no other blend, plus we liken the by-hand and by-heart production at Glenturret to the skills involved in the blending of The Famous Grouse'. In 2015, Edrington relaunched its Glenturret branded single malt to the market to wide fanfare and acclaim. Well worth a try.

A few words on The Glenturret distillery, which I was fortunate enough to visit last in late 2014, and loved…

Much of the distillery process is recognisable as that of virtually all others, but once in the mashing room I started to see and feel what made The Glenturret different, what made it interesting and how it's quirkiness lives in the people working here.

Glenturret is the only remaining hand-operated mash in the industry. Three quantities of water are poured through the mash; this is the part of the process that breaks down starches in the barley to kick-start the fermentation process, all the while preserving the enzymes that will fuel the flavour a few years down the line. As the water is poured in, a mashman hand-sifts, works and moves the mash around with great difficulty.

Why? Partly for tourism and partly to keep up the traditions of the brand's forefathers. It is true that it takes longer, but it gets the mash sugar content down to about 0.5 per cent, which is less than most others and is wildly consistent across batches. The Glenturret see a maximum variation of 1 per cent across batches.

There are no computers at Glenturret; rather a wonderful sense of this place capturing distilling as it should be done, and brought to life succinctly in its latest brand expression: 'By heart and by hand'.

For me, the original The Famous Grouse characterises how a mass-market whisky should be: enjoyable, inoffensive and highly sippable. If it were not any or all of these, there is no way that three drams of The Famous Grouse would be enjoyed in Scotland every second. That's pretty impressive.

Glenturret is the only remaining hand-operated mash in the industry

SCOTLAND'S
OLDEST
DISTILLERY

ESTABLISHED
1775

THE BRAND'S ICONIC ADVERTISING

Cast your mind back to the eighties and nineties – or look it up on YouTube if you weren't there – and see if you can remember The Famous Grouse jingle. That little melody is now firmly stuck in my head as I write this…do do do do do-do do do. A far cry from the epic adverts depicting the 'pioneering spirit' of Glenfiddich or the turbulent seafaring, windswept and evocative adverts of Talisker Storm and Dark Storm, this is light-hearted and smile-raising. No matter the similarities or differences, each brand requires its adverts to play a different role, changing the pace of the category for consumers and allowing them to buy into many ideas in just one whisky, from rugged weather-beaten areas to the endeavours of mankind.

When you get beneath the surface, The Famous Grouse has a very credible and interesting range, including The Famous Grouse Smoky Black (formerly The Black Grouse), The Famous Grouse Mellow Gold, The Naked Grouse, The Famous Grouse 16 Year Old and The Famous Grouse Alpha Edition.

When you get beneath the surface, The Famous Grouse has a very credible and interesting range

Right: Bespoke wallpaper in the visitor centre of The Glenturret.

Below: Cask end in The Glenturret Distillery.

Facing page: Stunning old The Famous Grouse bottles.

Why I chose this chapter's suggested whisky

For me The Famous Grouse 16 Year Old is the most impressive visually, with a gorgeous illustrated secondary pack (box) by Vic Lee encasing the spirit in opulent purple packaging, embellished with gold illustrations of the grouse. Note, this is a limited edition and may not be available everywhere; duty-free is your best bet for obtaining this whisky as it stands.

You immediately get a sense that The Famous Grouse 16 Year Old is grown up; it stands tall having been matured in first-fill Spanish sherry casks and first-fill American bourbon casks. The liquid is bright gold in colour, the nose is potent but not overly powerful, and the palate exudes nutmeg, cinnamon and a soft vanilla undertone and is very spicy throughout.

THE
FAMOUS
GROUSE

DOUBLE MATURED
BLENDED SCOTCH WHISKY

AGED 16 YEARS

FROM Sherry &
BOURBON CASKS
AGED 16 YEARS

THE SWEETENED COUNTENANCES
OF CARAMELISED Pears ACQUAINT
WITH DEEP BLACK Cherries
To SMILES & BEAUTY

Facing page: Grouse iron work at The Glenturret Distillery.

Above: The stunning artwork for The Famous Grouse 16 Year Old.

Right: Greg blending his first limited edition '1 of 1' bottle of whisky… a great experience in a fantastically designed The Famous Grouse archive and blending room.

CHAPTER SIX

CHIVAS BROTHERS

Suggested whisky:

Chivas 25 Year Old

This is getting to be a familiar story when talking about the early years of Scotch: grocers expanding their businesses to become bottlers and blenders of whisky. The Chivas strand of the story is no different.

In 1841, James Chivas acquired a grocery store in Aberdeen, along with around five years of experience in delivering great customer service, a relative novelty of the day, and a refined sales technique. Partnering with Charles Stewart, another shop owner in the area, the two specialised in both wine and spirits, and later in the 1850s with blended Scotch, under the Royal Glen Dee brand. This evolved into their flagship product once their reputation for high quality, consistent and smooth-drinking products had spread across the land.

James had been awarded a Royal Warrant in 1843 following a steadily growing demand from Queen Victoria as she entertained at the Balmoral Estate. The business grew over the following thirteen years until Chivas moved on from Stewart and formed a new partnership with his brother, John, and the Chivas Brothers brand, product and icon was born.

Sadly, John had passed away by 1862, but his name lived on in the brand and the name of the stores. The stores did well and ticked over nicely, but the Chivas Brothers' blends became the focus of their business as its revenues grew and grew, with Alexander Chivas taking over operations in 1886 when James also passed away.

This is getting to be a familiar story when talking about the early years of Scotch: grocers expanding their businesses to become bottlers and blenders of whisky. The Chivas strand of the story is no different

During the last thirty years of his life, James Chivas had been squirrelling away casks, laying them down for creating what he saw as his crowning achievement, the most luxurious blended Scotch in the world. Alexander kept this ethos of laying down stock and ageing their spirit for long periods of time, and upon his ultimate passing, at the young age of thirty-seven, the business was left in the hands of another partnership, Alexander Smith and Charles Stewart Howard, who ultimately created the Chivas Regal blend and brand.

They entered America in a big way, with the American desire for premium packaging and what would become known as strong provenance cues inspiring the outline look and feel of the brand we, and Chivas Regal consumers in 149 other markets around the world, all know and love with over four and a half million cases of Chivas Regal being sold globally each year. And that's despite prohibition killing off American exports for the brand for several years until the brand relaunched Stateside with the Chivas Regal 12 Year Old blend.

THE FIRST LUXURY SCOTCH WHISKY

One of the brand's biggest claims to fame, and why the current iteration has been chosen as the dram of choice for this chapter, is creating what it claims to be 'the world's first luxury Scotch whisky' with its Chivas Regal 25 Year Old.

The flavour profile of the Chivas blend is all about being silky-smooth, with a rich character that delivers the brand promise of being a super-premium blend, with expressions that pull apart different key flavours and explore the profiles possible within blended Scotch.

As with all mega brands in the blended Scotch world, Chivas was then bought, sold and bought again, first by Seagram in 1949, then eventually by Pernod Ricard.

The flavour profile of the Chivas blend is all about being silky-smooth, with a rich character that delivers the brand promise of being a super-premium blend

The rarely acknowledged Strathisla distillery in Speyside produces the backbone malt component to the blend, and also happens to be the oldest operating distillery in the Highlands, dating back 230 years. That's only ten years less than the United States of America has been independent from Great British rule.

What I love about Chivas Regal is one of its timeless, and still heralded, campaigns entitled 'Live with Chivalry', which ensured the Chivas brand was seen as a premium, luxurious blend enjoyed by those who embody values that society has, or had, lost over the years: honour, loyalty and gallantry.

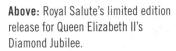

Above: Royal Salute's limited edition release for Queen Elizabeth II's Diamond Jubilee.

Left: The stunning view over the coast of Scotland as you come in to land in Aberdeen Airport on the way to Speyside; makes the 6am flight all the more worth it.

CHIVAS' "REGAL"

Unexcelled.

Gentlemen!   The Verdict.

"Unexcelled" means that which surpasses others in good qualities, laudable actions or acquirements, that which is distinguished by superiority. Here then you understand why there is a growing demand for

REGAL,

THE 25 YEAR OLD,

SCOTCH LIQUEUR WHISKY.

Pre-War Quality and Strength.

REGAL—a wealth of meaning, Gentlemen, and so easy to say—**REGAL.**

THE MORNING MIST lifts at a corrie's edge. Revealed, a 'Royal' and its hinds stand poised for flight. The flavour of such exciting moments is the flavour of Scotland—and so is the splendid taste of Chivas Regal Scotch Whisky. More than a century-and-a-half of tradition shapes the making of Chivas Regal—an inspired blend of Scotland's finest grain and malt whiskies, matured for 12 years before bottling. Such a superb whisky costs more, naturally. Discerning people gladly pay more. For here you taste the glory of the Prince of Whiskies—that magnificent something extra that's the regal flavour of Scotland.

SCOTLAND'S PRINCE OF WHISKIES

CHIVAS REGAL

12-YEARS-OLD 75° proof **54/6**

You either have it   or you don't

AS LONG AS A NOBLE HEART CAN BE RECOGNIZED NO MATTER WHAT THE DISGUISE ...

There will always be a

CHIVAS REGAL.

The links between Chivas, chivalry and the company's ethos have forged strong messaging platforms over the years, empowering new generations with the tools needed to show their chivalrous side to the opposite sex, with a nod to 'winning in the right way', not just winning by any means available. This more recent expression of the campaign coincided with global competition The Venture, where start-ups could win a share of $1million to help make their innovative idea a reality.

Indeed, Chivas Brothers are not afraid to continue making changes to the way it talks to whisky lovers, in line with changing trends. In 2010 the brand launched its 'Age Matters' campaign in response to research that stated 94 per cent of consumers believed an age statement served as an indicator of quality. The campaign encouraged consumers to look for a number on their bottles, emphasising the belief that age was a crucial component to a great whisky. However, with demand rising and whisky lovers' knowledge across the globe constantly increasing, Chivas Regal has not been afraid to introduce new expressions that go beyond age signifiers to signal quality, having launched a number of NAS releases including Chivas Regal Extra and Chivas Regal Ultis.

To its credit, that specific campaign did evolve into 'Great Things Take Time', likely in reaction to brands such as The Macallan, The Glenlivet, Highland Park, Glenfiddich et al all releasing products without age-denoting numbers on the bottle.

Above: I love this poster; a truly classic advert for an iconic product.

Facing page (left): A selection of the iconic adverts Chivas Brothers have produced over the years.

The rarely acknowledged Strathisla distillery in Speyside produces the backbone malt component to the blend, and also happens to be the oldest operating distillery in the Highlands, dating back 230 years

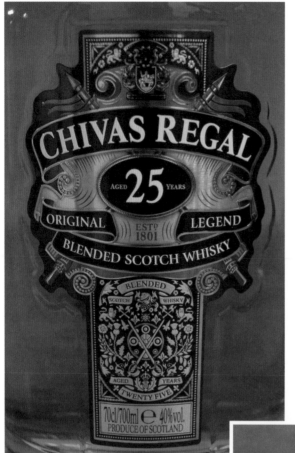

Why I chose this chapter's suggested whisky

As the first 'luxury' whisky, I had high hopes. And does it deliver? My God, it does. So silky smooth, and with a recipe that is nuanced each year based on supply and availability of spirit in the Chivas Brothers warehouses, it has a note that is reminiscent of a zesty chocolate orange, if you can imagine such a thing, milk chocolate creaminess maybe.

Wrapped with a subtle wisp of smoke, a nutty marzipan note is present, reminiscent of the old school Christmas cake your mother used to make, complete with sweetness from the icing and dark fruit notes drawn from sherry casks, but all the roundedness you'd expect from bourbon casks. A fantastic whisky that I love spending time with, time and time again. It must have really blown the minds of whisky drinkers when it was first released.

IT'S GREAT DRAMS WHISKY TASTING TIME

Think about the nose and palate…
What notes are you getting? Is it…
Sweet? Sour? Smoky? Spicy?
Summer fruits? Winter fruits?
Oakiness? All of these?
None of these?

Try to decode what your nose and palate
are telling you – everyone's experience
with whisky is personal and can
vary so feel free to explore and
understand your senses…

Your notes

_____   _____
_____   _____
_____   _____
_____   _____
_____   _____
_____   _____

**Remember to tell me how you get on with each whisky from the book on
Twitter, Facebook and Instagram: #GreatDramsOfScotland**

 **/GreatDrams** **@GreatDrams**  **greatdramsgreg**

THE MYTHS & LEGENDS

CHAPTER SEVEN

PORT ELLEN

Suggested whisky:

Port Ellen 24 Year Old, distilled in 1978
(The second release in the Diageo Special Releases)

Oh Port Ellen, the legendary dead Islay distillery heralded as one of the best producers of Islay malt in the mid to latter part of the last century by many a whisky commentator.

I only own one Port Ellen bottle, one of the Diageo Special Releases that was distilled in 1978 and bottled at twenty-four years old. I opened it for Christmas 2015 to celebrate a wonderful year of GreatDrams, which included my first invitation to the launch of the Diageo Special Releases. The 2015 release was the immense Port Ellen 32 Year Old.

Yes. Yes. Yes. Oh yes. I always thought this was going to be a hero of a dram, and I was not disappointed one bit. This delightfully dark Port Ellen release gave myself, and a few others who sampled it with me, a near-sensual experience. Oodles of Port Ellen smokiness and dark fruits interweave to create something truly special. Beneath the surface there are waves of fruit,

honey and spices that create a perfectly balanced whisky that I could genuinely nose all night.

Then, at my second Diageo Special Releases event in September 2016, I was very fortunate to try the oldest Port Ellen bottled to date, a 37 Year Old whopper of a dram. On initial taste I was actually pretty dubious – there was something missing for me – but following discussion with Chris 'Tiger' White of the Edinburgh Whisky Blog, and a second and third sip, we started to get on quite well. The complexity grows and grows on you, with sweet peat wrapped in smoked, maybe cured, meats with just a small amount of heat to it. Quite a savoury Port Ellen release with a long, gentle herbaceous finish. After a stuttering start in our short friendship, I really warmed up to it. This 2,940 limited-edition cask-strength release was from a marriage of refill American Oak hogsheads and refill European Oak butts that were filled in 1978.

A PIONEERING DISTILLERY THAT SADLY FELL SILENT

Dating back to 1825, when A K Mackay & Co. set the site up as a malt mill, it has come full circle and is now known as Port Ellen Maltings and services the malt needs of most of the distilleries on Islay. The distillery itself was converted, rightly so, into a distillery by a chap named John Ramsey, a local Member of Parliament and clearly also a wise man, in 1836.

Port Ellen was also, allegedly, as notes the commemorative book that companied the 2016 Special Releases launch, the first distillery to trade with America, in 1848, securing the right to use larger casks than were typical of the time for storage in bonded duty-free warehouses ahead of export, something that continues to this day.

Port Ellen was also apparently the first to make use of the spirit safe, a storage facility invented by Septimus Fox in the 1820s. Copious romantic stories exist about spirit safes throughout the industry, but the truth is that the practical use of them is to enable the examination of fresh, new-make spirit without exposing it to the atmosphere. Optional at first, spirit safes were made compulsory in 1823 following the introduction of the Excise Act, where one set of keys were held at the distillery and one by Her Majesty's Revenue & Customs to prevent illicit distilling and avoidance of tax.

Ramsey is owed a degree of thanks by many blenders the world over for his work with Aeneas Coffey and Robert Stein. Between them,

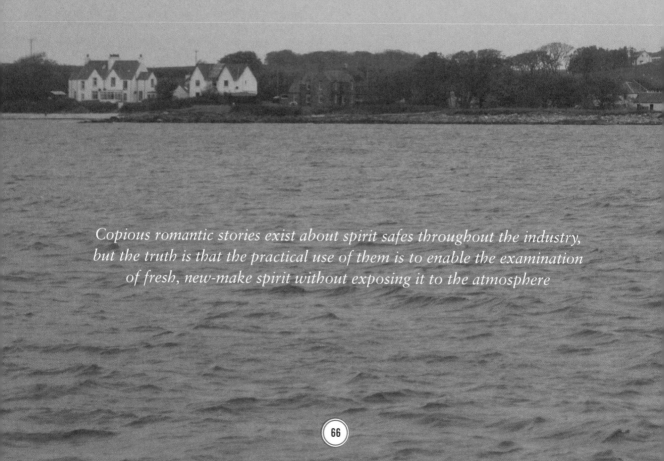

Copious romantic stories exist about spirit safes throughout the industry, but the truth is that the practical use of them is to enable the examination of fresh, new-make spirit without exposing it to the atmosphere

they developed innovative continuous stills that were later installed at the Port Ellen distillery. As with many distilleries over the last couple of hundred years, the Ramsey family retained the distillery after the founder's death, but after a couple of decades they sold to a bigger player. In this case, initially John Dewar and Sons, in 1920, later merging with DCL in 1925 and temporarily closing in 1929.

During this time the ownership was transferred to Scottish Malt Distillers, and the maltings and bonded warehouse continued to be operated as usual, servicing the rest of the distilleries on the island of Islay. Eventually, Port Ellen reopened as a distillery around 1966 and 1967, with two new stills added to the production line.

The distillery then produced and filled spirit throughout the seventies, with the warehousemen and stillmen of the time having no idea how the spirit would mature through the following decades as it was not really designed to be kept in cask for that long. I'm also certain that they, like virtually everyone else, had no idea what a globally sought-after whisky each Port Ellen distillery release would become.

Sadly, this revival only lasted sixteen years, until 1983, when the distillery was finally mothballed and dismantled due to a decline in Scotch consumption during the preceding decade. Despite not being operational any more, its legend still lives on today and will live on long into tomorrow owing to the quality of the product it used to produce, and the spectacular PR and taste profile around every limited release from this dead distillery's diminishing stockpile.

Islay pilgrims can still see the iconic Port Ellen warehouses emblazoned with the distillery's name; this is the case for most distilleries on Islay because they were originally built by the coast. Aside from the warehouses, you cannot see any more of the distillery buildings belonging to Port Ellen. However, a useful heads-up is that the maltings, usually only open to press and trade, is open to the public during the Islay Festival every year.

The 2015 Port Ellen Diageo Special Releases bottling launched at an eye-watering £2,400 but, as Nick Morgan, Diageo's head of whisky outreach, has said for a number of years, there is no more Port Ellen in production, so once it is gone, it really is gone.

I do wonder how much stock they have left…

If the prices of Port Ellen are a bit steep, take a look at the Caol Ila range as, in both my opinion and that of others in the whisky-writing world, it is the closest in character to what you'd expect from a Port Ellen release, and a very underrated distillery.

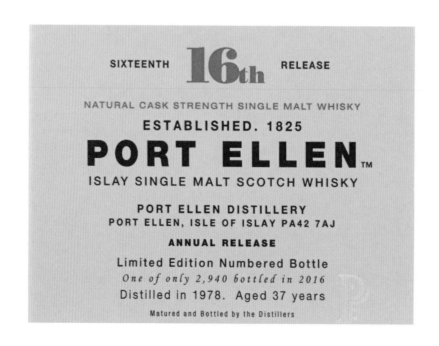

Why I chose this chapter's suggested whisky

Well that's a simple one to answer: Port Ellen 24 Year Old distilled in 1978, the second release in the Diageo Special Releases, was the first bottle of Port Ellen I owned. Bought from a Bonhams' whisky auction for £750, it was the first Port Ellen I had seen in about three years sell for less than four figures, so I convinced myself it was a bargain…and I still believe this to be the case. The bottle itself, number 570 of 12,000, was only the second of the Port Ellen Diageo Special Releases bottled at 59.35% in 2002, and it's pretty damn special.

The nose gives off sweet honey notes with a light underpinning of peat you'd expect from an Islay single malt; it's salty too. On the palate, the whisky really opens up, more peat is present, the taste a little bitter, still salty, this time tropical fruit. The dram has a very long finish; this is a truly complex drink which I enjoy spending time with.

Note, if you are unable to obtain this suggested whisky, opt for the latest Caol Ila Distillers Edition release.

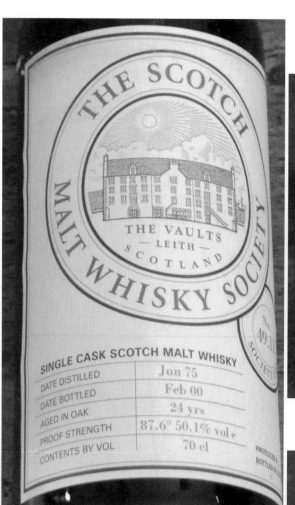

THE SCOTCH
MALT WHISKY SOCIETY

THE VAULTS
— LEITH —
SCOTLAND

No.
49.11
SOCIETY

SINGLE CASK SCOTCH MALT WHISKY

DATE DISTILLED	Jun 75
DATE BOTTLED	Feb 00
AGED IN OAK	24 yrs
PROOF STRENGTH	87.6° 50.1% vol e
CONTENTS BY VOL	70 cl

PRODUCED &
BOTTLED IN

CHAPTER EIGHT

ST. MAGDALENE

Suggested whisky:

SMWS 49.11, a St. Magdalene 27 Year Old

It took a while for me to try my first dram of St. Magdalene. My first sip was on 29 May 2015 at 10.47 a.m., to be precise, when a lovely man named Ian Hunter, whom I had met at the Islay Festival, happened to be attending the same 'breakfast whisky tasting' as me.

We got on famously and enjoyed the scheduled drams that morning, after a hearty fry-up I hasten to add. A little later, for reasons unbeknown to me, Ian whipped out a bottle of SMWS 49.11, a St. Magdalene 27 Year Old distilled in June 1975. I did not complain, obviously. In fact, I was instantly in love, as you will see in the whisky notes on page 73.

Now you know of my love for the whisky, one of the old Lowland malts, I should probably tell you about the brand and the distillery itself.

Adam Dawson, the founder of St. Magdalene and a former brewer, obtained his licence in 1797. St. Magdalene was officially opened in 1798, making it one of the first legal distilleries in Scotland, although there are credible accounts from around that time that the distillery was operating illicitly from 1765 by a fellow called Sebastian Henderson.

Originally named Linlithgow, after the town in which it was situated, several releases from the distillery were sent to market under that name and can still be found on the internet today – although not many! This town also happened to be where Mary Queen of Scots was born.

As an aside, legend has it Mary Queen of Scots was responsible for two iconic British staples still enjoyed today: marmalade and the Bloody Mary. Legendary Master Distiller Richard Paterson once told me that when Mary Queen of Scots was beheaded, it took three attempts to cut off her head, with blood going everywhere, and that this fact formed the basis of why the future cocktail was so named.

As an aside, Mary also happened to get very sea sick when travelling and was given marmalade, a rare delicacy at the time, as it was the only thing that made her feel well again. The word marmalade deriving from the French term 'Marie malade', meaning 'sick Mary'. Granted, this has been disputed over the years, but I like to believe this version.

Back to St. Magdalene...

The site itself was based on an old leper colony dating back to the twelfth century called St Magdalene's Cross, which was later converted into a convent named Lazar House.

In its day, and according to statistics published around the mid-eighteenth century, the distillery could produce 3,300 gallons of spirit per week. The Dawson family retained operational control right up until 1912, when they sadly went out of business, leaving the distillery silent for three years until the Scottish Distillers Company bought the brand and distillery.

The distillery remained as it was under the control of the Scottish Distillers Company, until a complete refit took place in 1927, adding both capacity and improved operational efficiency: essentially, better quality production and a lot more whisky.

The site itself was based on an old leper colony dating back to the twelfth century called St Magdalene's Cross, which was later converted into a convent named Lazar House

AN ELUSIVE, MYSTERIOUS DISTILLERY

St. Magdalene was one of the first distilleries to install drum maltings; this is the process of mechanically turning grain rather than turning it all by hand. But, like many distilleries, St. Magdalene ceased floor malting in 1967 when it became cheaper to buy malt in from third-party suppliers and, just sixteen years later, in 1983, the whole distillery was mothballed.

Throughout its 185 year official history, the majority of the whisky produced and matured here went into blended Scotch and very little into single malt bottlings, making the bottles you can find on the web and at auctions even rarer. Diageo releases the odd bottle through its Special Releases range, and an occasional bottle released by independent bottlers, such as Douglas Laing, pops up, but in reality there cannot be much St. Magdalene left.

Sadly, only the pagoda-style roofs remain from the St. Magdalene distillery site as most of the site was converted into flats in the 1990s, which is such a shame. Regardless, the memory of this distillery will live on through very rare bottlings that I'm confident everyone will enjoy sipping.

Why I chose this chapter's suggested whisky

As mentioned, SMWS 49.11, a St. Magdalene 27 Year Old, is spectacular. This buttery beauty is so soft and sublime, yet has a depth to it that, when I tasted it, I don't think I had experienced for a while, if ever. It is one I've fondly remembered and, to this day, I have been looking out for a special release from this long-lost distillery to keep in the cabinet for special times.

CHAPTER NINE

KININVIE

Suggested whisky:

Kininvie 23 Year Old, Batch Two

Dubbed 'the most reclusive distillery in Scotland', only trade and press are allowed to visit this elusive distillery and no photos are allowed. My only visit thus far was more or less by accident whilst visiting the Glenfiddich distillery for Burn's Night 2014. Kininvie is a dark horse; it is up to you whether or not you wish to tame it or ride it.

It was a refreshing sight I must say, to see a distillery not looking for attention and not trying to be something more than what it is: an industrious installation on the flowing landscape of Dufftown, Speyside.

The operations are still manual, as they are at distilleries such as Laphroaig, Ardbeg, Glenfiddich and some notable others, and the stills sit almost smiling now they are getting the attention they deserve for the spirit they have created for just over a quarter of a century.

The Kininvie distillery was opened in 1990 by Janet Sheed Roberts, the last remaining granddaughter of William Grant, to primarily supply malt for Balvenie, Glenfiddich and the third largest blended Scotch brand in the world: Grant's. Kininvie also forms one of three components in the Monkey Shoulder vatted malt (the other two being Glenfiddich and Balvenie), but its flavour profile has, to this day, remained largely a family secret.

Located right next to its sister distilleries, mentioned above, the Kininvie distillery is all hand operated, but it is also able to run with just a single operator and a computer. Don't be fooled though; this is not a cold, industrial place.

Kininvie is a dark horse; it is up to you whether or not you wish to tame it or ride it

Above: The instantly iconic Kininvie bottle packaging; evocative of place, mysterious by nature and with so many design layers it is a really interesting case study for packaging design.

It looks more like a cow shed than a distillery, with a still house made of three corrugated walls and a transparent one, and no wash or mash house to be seen. It is actually the furthest away from the still house of any distillery in Scotland, William Grant & Sons' global whisky specialist Kevin Abrook informed me, and is housed in a building with The Balvenie's wash and mash houses, although completely separate, as it has to be by law. Kininvie itself is tiny.

The first single malt Scotch whisky from the distillery to bear the Kininvie name was launched as a 23 Year Old Batch One exclusively in Taiwan in 2013. A few months later, in early 2014, a 23 Year Old Batch Two was released in the UK and Nordic countries.

Prior to this, a couple of William Grant & Sons employee exclusive bottlings took place under the Halewood name, Hazelwood 105 and Hazelwood Reserve 107. These were released in celebration of the aforementioned Janet Sheed Roberts' birthdays – she lived to an incredible 110 years old.

Speaking ahead of the launch of the Kininvie 25 Year Old 'The First Drops' release, Craig Cranmer, the Kininvie's distillery manager, stated:

'Kininvie is something of a hidden gem. We have cherished and nurtured the casks for twenty-five years knowing they contained incredible whisky. Now the time is right to share the first drops of our history, straight from the casks where they have been maturing since the distillery's first days.'

IT'S ALL IN THE PACKAGING

This brand has created something really special with its packaging. The bottle itself is all about crafting a mysterious look and feel for the most mysterious of distilleries. Layered, interesting and exactly how the distillery should be encapsulated.

Brilliance, as always, is in the detail. And here I'm looking at the 23 Year Old Batch Two release.

You'll notice that the brand identity (that's consultant speak for logo) wraps around the secondary packaging (more consultant speak, this time meaning the box) to give a sense of question-raising, of doing things differently, of being just that bit more interesting than the rest.

Another note on the brand identity; notice how the V and the I are underlined and treated slightly differently? That's a subtle nod to how many stills there are at the distillery – but don't tell anyone I told you.

The front of the secondary pack communicates that this is 'The Second House Release from the Kininvie Distillery' and that this is Batch Two aged twenty-three years. Aside from that, this outer pack is bare and intriguing.

Then you open it up…

Thick-stock grey tracing paper lies sealed with a white small batch sticker and a short brand story is written in punchy red, drawing you in and telling you enough to build the excitement but not to reveal all. Underneath this delicate shroud you finally see the bottle, and, wow, was the wait worth it.

It may only be 35cl but the bottle stands proud in a box of such quality that it is protected from any assumed harm. With a pull of a black ribbon gently surrounding the bottle, it pops out from its cradle and into your hands.

The label is very simple, grid-like, functional and almost medicinal in design. If you get a chance to buy, or even hold, this box and bottle, make sure you take the opportunity to rotate the bottle and look at the back of the label at eye level: the mirroring effect of the glass and liquid bring to life the chalkboard used to this day in the distillery to denote batch times, temperatures and a whole host of details that go into making this incredible single malt.

The front label details the age, the year of distillation, features approval signatures from the distillery manager and malt master, displays the bottle number and talks of the finish you will enjoy when you eventually sip this amber nectar.

Why I chose this chapter's suggested whisky

I guess we all know the answer to this one: Kininvie 23 Year Old, Batch Two is gorgeous. I will leave you to discover and dissect this one on your own because I fear I would not do it justice, as I always get too excited when my attention turns to Kininvie. Suffice to say, I enjoyed every single drop of that dram. A rare one that lives up to and beats the hype.

IT'S GREAT DRAMS WHISKY TASTING TIME

Think about the nose and palate…
What notes are you getting? Is it…
Sweet? Sour? Smoky? Spicy?
Summer fruits? Winter fruits?
Oakiness? All of these?
None of these?

Try to decode what your nose and palate
are telling you – everyone's experience
with whisky is personal and can
vary so feel free to explore and
understand your senses…

Your notes

_____   _____
_____   _____
_____   _____
_____   _____
_____   _____

**Remember to tell me how you get on with each whisky from the book on
Twitter, Facebook and Instagram: #GreatDramsOfScotland**

 **/GreatDrams**    **@GreatDrams**    **greatdramsgreg**

THE CLASSICS

CHAPTER TEN

THE MACALLAN

Suggested whisky:

The Macallan Rare Cask

As one of the first distilleries in the Speyside region to legally produce spirit for ageing into whisky, The Macallan distillery is a very special place. I'm sure a lot of you will agree with me that visiting this distillery is a pilgrimage for any whisky enthusiast.

Most distillery sites are specifically designed for distilling – sounds obvious, doesn't it? The Macallan distillery is so much more. On the estate they own 1.5 miles of the River Spey, complete with fishing, and stunning scenic views.

Despite being the whisky of James Bond, 007, The Macallan, like all distilleries pre-2010, was born of humble beginnings. In 1824 Alexander Reid, a local farmer, leased a modest eight acres from the Earl of Seafield to establish The Macallan distillery. From there a legend blossomed into the global icon with twenty-two warehouses we now know and love.

I was last there as a guest of the distillery's owners, Edrington, in 2015. Tours of this respect-commanding place are intimate, all questions are welcomed and encouraged – and I asked a fair few of my superb guide Ian during the couple of hours we spent walking around.

The biggest outtake from my visit was how incredibly interactive the place is. It's not like the other luxury brands such as Rolex, Louis Vuitton and Prada; The Macallan is a lot more down to earth and conversational, similar to Omega, Oakley and Audi. It is clear as you walk around that they want you to leave with the full understanding of not only the brand but the process of making whisky too, and have left

Despite being the whisky of James Bond, 007, The Macallan,
like all distilleries pre-2010, was born of humble beginnings

no stone unturned on this quest to educate every guest they receive at their brand's home.

Gorgeous brass and copper props with supporting screens are complemented by expensive installations of casks demonstrating each stage of their creation, from seasoning to maturation. A few metres ahead is a beautifully designed wall of essential oils to get your nose anticipating the different tasting notes you might get from future drams from The Macallan.

Nothing seems to be a greater source of pride for the brand than the level of quality control that goes into the cask side of The Macallan's production. The average age of the trees Edrington is felling in Spain is 110 years old, each one having enough good wood for four-

500 litre casks. Before you gasp in horror, the company is also planting trees quicker than it is cutting them down, netting a positive impact on the environment.

The European Oak used for its casks is first filled with sherry by the González Byass Bodega in Jerez, Spain. These casks typically cost five to ten times as much as the bourbon ones used by around 85–90 per cent of whisky producers (including The Macallan for some products).

Once cut, the oak is left to air-dry for two years, before it is toasted and seasoned for two years with sherry and finally shipped whole. This process effectively sacrifices space on the shipping vessel in order to ship casks with air in them all the way to Scotland; that way a quality check can

Above: Easter Elchies House sitting at the heart of The Macallan Estate.

Left: A very old bottle of The Macallan.

Below: Casks 'sleeping' at the distillery.

The average age of the trees Edrington is felling in Spain is 110 years old, each one having enough good wood for four-500 litre casks

take place there ahead of filling and maturing.

To give a little context, that means creating a 12 Year Old bottle of The Macallan whisky takes at least eighteen years when you factor in the oak cutting, drying, seasoning, distilling, filling and maturation period.

Good job the company are building the new distillery, then: current demand is so high that The Macallan are full to the rafters with 220,000 casks occupying warehouses with a maximum capacity of 250,000. The new distillery under construction should mean we don't have to panic about The Macallan running dry just yet.

HIGH END, HIGH FINISH, HIGHLY ABSORBING

I have been to quite a few distilleries in my time and can honestly say that there were elements of the process I've been told about many times before, for example the inner workings of the stills, that only clicked when I saw the visual representations and miniature installations, such as the scale models at The Macallan.

The Macallan also happens to be one of the last distilleries to marry its whisky in spent

sherry casks. This process takes nine months for the older vintages and must cost a fortune as the casks take up so much space! The result is a whisky with all inputs working together in perfect harmony.

The brand has spent a lot of time defining the six pillars, a set of beliefs and ways of being that defines what it means to be The Macallan.

Here is a bit of detail on the six pillars, with the help of The Macallan brand book:

The Macallan also happens to be one of the last distilleries to marry its whisky in spent sherry casks... The result is a whisky with all inputs working together in perfect harmony

1. Spiritual Home

Easter Elchies House, built in 1700, lies at the heart of The Macallan estate.

Dating back over 300 years and built out of locally quarried sandstone, The Macallan estate spans 390 acres, 90 of which are sown each year using their proprietary strain of barley, Minstrel.

The River Spey borders the estate, sheep scatter the surrounding fields and highland cattle roam free.

2. Curiously Small Stills

The smallest stills in Speyside, the twenty-one stills that make up The Macallan production are so designed to allow maximum contact between spirit and copper, creating the rich, fruity and full-bodied flavours we all know and love from The Macallan. Scottish readers may or may not know this, but The Macallan stills previously featured on the back of your £10 note.

3. Finest Cut

Every distillery divides their spirit throughout the process, with the resulting 'cut' being collected and filled into casks for maturation.

The Macallan only uses fine cut of every run to ensure they capture the character you'd expect from the brand, whilst developing an incredibly oily new-make spirit which comes off the stills at 69.8% before being filled in casks.

4. Exceptional Oak Casks

I've spoken about the commitment to oak of The Macallan and Edrington. The practicalities of this are evident in The Macallan's commissioned research which found that up to 80 per cent of the flavour in whisky comes from the contact and reaction between spirit and oak, leading Edrington to invest significantly more in wood every year than any other single malt producer.

According to the brand itself, The Macallan spends more on sourcing, building, seasoning and caring for its casks than any other single malt whisky. I have no way of confirming this, but it is a bold claim and one that shows its commitment to being and producing the best of the best whisky.

Left: One of my favourite distillery photos; snowy barrels making an industrial process look picturesque.

Right, top: Behind the scenes at The Macallan Distillery.

Right, bottom: Some super-expensive expressions in The Macallan gift shop... one day...

5. Natural Colour

Should be a given, no? Well yes, but in many cases whiskies get coloured to fit perceptions of darker whiskies, which symbolise superior quality. At The Macallan there is none of that. All is natural and all is gorgeous.

From light to incredibly dark mahogany, what you see is exactly how it came out of the casks.

6. The Macallan Itself

As a brand guy and a romantic, I love the term 'peerless spirit' and could not agree more. There is something special here, something unique, and whilst I've written a lot of words on it, there is also something inexplicable about both the brand and product that you will only truly understand once you visit the distillery and spend time with the whiskies in the place they were created.

Above: Spent casks used for marrying the matured whisky together into a harmonious single malt.

Why I chose this chapter's suggested whisky

The Macallan Rare Cask is the pinnacle of The Macallan's mainstream releases. This whisky is a marriage of sixteen different sherry-cask styles in what the Edrington group describe as 'a whisky crafted from casks so rare they will never again be used in any Macallan whisky', this nectar is all about the sherry colour and flavour profile.

Having first tried The Macallan Rare Cask at a whisky show, I love it. Personally, I think, at £190 (at the time of writing) this is an incredible bargain

to be had – in fact, I was so enthralled, I bought one that evening.

The nose smells as if you had been transported back to the warehouses where these casks had been sleeping all these years: quite spicy, with deep sherry and coffee notes.

The palate is all about warming, relaxed notes highlighting dried fruits, caramel and chocolate. A very fine, very mature whisky, it's one I savour every time I pour myself a dram.

CHAPTER ELEVEN

LAPHROAIG

Now, I've often described Laphroaig as my 'spiritual home' in whisky, which has a lot to do with the iconic Laphroaig 10 being the whisky that convinced me that drinking and exploring whisky was a good idea and that it should be enjoyed and savoured – although I'm not ashamed to admit that it took a few efforts to get on board with a whisky that, at the time, was the peatiest I had ever tried.

It would be remiss of me not to publicly thank my good friend Anthony Collyer who persisted with me until I loved sipping the stuff without wincing. Since working within the industry, I have heard from many sources, from brand ambassadors to journalists to authors and production folk, that they had the exact same experience as I (albeit not with Anthony pestering them to 'man up' each time they sampled this

fine malt, I imagine).

Laphroaig itself is Gaelic for 'the beautiful hollow by the broad bay'. Having been to the distillery a few times now, I have heard many stories, but my favourite fact is that Laphroaig was one of the only, if not the only, Scotch that was allowed to be sold in America during the 1920–1933 prohibition on alcohol. This was made possible by the ever-inventive whisky folk who managed to get the Surgeon General to list it as 'medicinal spirit' after deciding that 'no one would drink this stuff for pleasure'. Clearly not a peat-head.

Ahead of being sold to Long John Distillers in the early 1960s, the distillery was owned by the Johnston family for well over a century. In the 1920s the final family member made their most significant hiring in someone now regarded

Laphroaig itself is Gaelic for 'the beautiful hollow by the broad bay'

as not only an innovator within the industry but a true whisky legend: Bessie Williamson.

Bessie originally came to work in the distillery for just one summer, as a receptionist, but ended up staying for forty years, becoming instrumental in the expansion of the business, and the building of the brand we know and love today.

What led to a summer secretary becoming such a prominent figure in what is now the biggest of the Islay single malts? She was a thinker, both practically and creatively. Her work ethic and curiosity about distilling, not only at the distillery but as assistant to her predecessor-to-be Ian Hunter after he had a stroke, led to her not only being promoted to distillery manager but being left the distillery in the final Johnston's final will. Years later, and not only was her Laphroaig brand building revered but also her charity work,

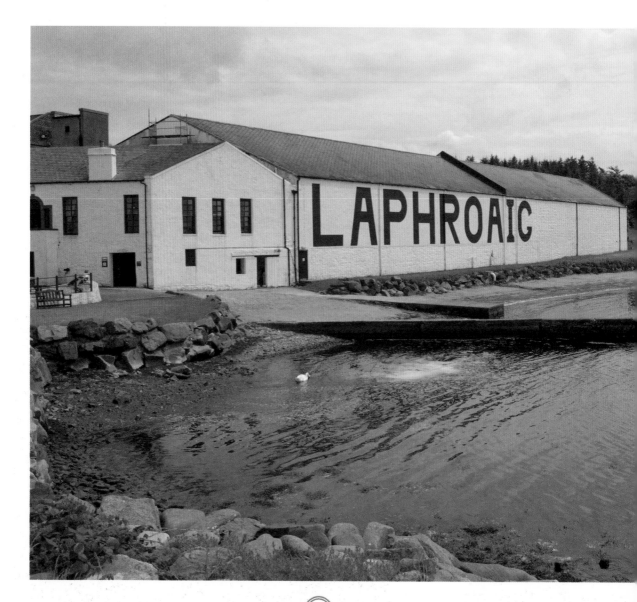

which lead to her being awarded the Order of St. John by The Queen in recognition of all she did.

Fast forward a few years and we are close to the modern Laphroaig story, having been acquired by Beam in 2005, and more recently Suntory in 2014. The latter has vowed not to interfere in the day-to-day distillery management and operations, but will use its global business to find new routes to market and to start new conversations with an increasing potential consumer base.

What led to a summer secretary becoming such a prominent figure in what is now the biggest of the Islay single malts? She was a thinker, both practically and creatively

Above: One of the hard-working stills at the Laphroaig Distillery.

Left: The stunning Laphroaig distillery; a photo every true whisky lover should take one day.

From a production perspective, very little barley is grown on the island any more; only the Kilchoman distillery still does, as they are a working farm with Bruichladdich releasing Islay Barley whiskies each year using barley from the island. Many of the other Islay distilleries buy in their barley from the Port Ellen maltings, owned by Diageo.

What stands Laphroaig aside, however, is its malting process. The brand is only one of seven in Scotland to still carry out its own drying and peating due to the expense, but it is unwilling to outsource the entirety of the process as it feels this could compromise the quality of the Laphroaig flavour, so instead do 15 per cent of the malting in-house.

To put this in perspective, the peat is all cut by hand (I know as I had a go at cutting it a couple of years ago as a birthday treat). This is preferred as even though it is left to dry for six to eight weeks, it is still soggy inside, which means it burns at a lower temperature so giving off more smoke when burnt to capture the renowned flavour of Laphroaig that we all enjoy once aged, bottled and consumed.

One of my favourite stories about Laphroaig is a tale told in bars around Islay from the time when HRH Prince Charles awarded the company

Left to right: Me working Laphroaig's peat bog on Islay; a great day; my wife and I enjoying a well-deserved dram of Laphroaig 18 Year Old after a few minutes grafting in the peat bog; a pile of peat bricks ready to be dried and used as fuel in the kiln; peat smoking in the Laphroaig kiln, adding flavour and aromatics to the malted barley.

a Royal Warrant in 1994. He was apparently a tad embarrassed having piloted and then crashed into the peat bog the plane in which he arrived, although the distillery tries to assure all they tell that he had not yet sampled Laphroaig's peaty goodness yet that day… You have to wonder.

Turns out that Laphroaig is Prince Charles's favourite whisky, hence the Royal Warrant, and he even bottles his own Laphroaig for charity events under his Highgrove brand.

Further into the production process, the brand uses stainless steel washbacks (these are the vessels where the fermentation stage takes place, turning the raw inputs into an alcoholic solution akin to beer) – like most distilleries they moved from wooden washbacks to stainless steel as they are easier to maintain and clean. The move is especially poignant given the old washbacks were rumoured to have the presence of the ghost of one of the Johnston family members, who leaned in too far and ended up drowning in the mash. Not a bad way to go, but not a great way either.

Turns out that Laphroaig is Prince Charles's favourite whisky, hence the Royal Warrant, and he even bottles his own Laphroaig for charity events under his Highgrove brand

LEGACY PROCESSES FROM A TIME LONG PAST

For some reason, as I'm sure you've gathered from other chapters, I'm always a sucker for a spirit safe; there's something gorgeous about what it stands for. And the spirit safe at Laphroaig is great, still operated completely manually using polished brass levers, hand turned when the time is right. The chunky customs-and-excise padlocks are also clearly visible.

I once asked Laphroaig's head of production why they never mechanised the process, I was told relatively bluntly: 'Why change something that works so well?' Fair enough.

Above: Proudly standing by the spirit safe in the Laphroaig Distillery.

Right: Spirit flowing from the Laphroaig stills.

Above: Some of the rarer Laphroaig casks, look closely at the one on the left, signed by HRH Prince Charles.

Ninety-five per cent of the Laphroaig spirit is matured in bourbon casks, most of these being shipped from the Maker's Mark distillery in Kentucky that are shipped to the Speyside Cooperage who rebuild them and send them on to Laphroaig.

Curiously, for a Scotch whisky brand, Laphroaig mostly uses its casks once, then they are sold to other producers and independent bottlers for finishing and blending.

Another interesting fact about Islay single malts I should probably mention is that, aside from Bruichladdich, they are all bottled on the mainland for onward distribution around the world.

Curiously, for a Scotch whisky brand, Laphroaig mostly uses its casks once, then they are sold to other producers and independent bottlers for finishing and blending

Laphroaig fill 3.5 million litres of spirit per year. Imagine the amount of storage needed just for new stock each year! Incredible. All its warehouses used to be cattle sheds, converted as and when they were needed for storage, with new purpose-built warehouses being built more recently as production has grown exponentially.

One day, if you visit Islay, ask about how Lagavulin came into being and the challenges that arose as Sir Peter Mackie tried to copy Laphroaig's style and product in the then newly created Malt Mill. I'm confident you'll be both surprised and intrigued to learn more.

To counter any threat of competition, Laphroaig bought the surrounding fields and hills in order to protect its water source – which is huge, by the way – and thus secure the future of the distillery. Laphroaig dedicated the fields to the Friends of Laphroaig who, with each bottle they purchase, can claim their square foot of land on the distillery's site and claim rent of a 5cl bottle of Laphroaig's 10 Year Old upon visiting.

Why I chose this chapter's suggested whisky

Oh yes, Laphroaig 10 Year Old Cask Strength, Batch 005 is not only my suggested whisky for this chapter, but my favourite whisky to date. I first tried it in the Ballygrant Inn on Islay in 2014 and it really rocked my world. I enjoyed it so much so that I immediately went online and bought not one but three bottles.

Distilled in 2003 and released in 2013, the ex-bourbon cask-matured whisky is stunning.

It is a 'pimped up' Laphroaig 10 Year Old that has an incredibly fresh nose, lots of barley and new-make waft through the air, along with honey and the vanilla notes expected from ex-bourbon casks. The palate is strong but welcoming: oodles of peat, bonfire notes, quite dry, salty and medicinal. Bloody lovely.

CHAPTER TWELVE

GLENFIDDICH

Suggested whisky:

Glenfiddich 18, one of my favourite Speysiders

Ah Glenfiddich: the grandfather of commercial single malt Scotch. Glenfiddich was founded by William Grant, a pioneer for the whisky industry. Over the years, subsequent generations have been equally pioneering, but that's skipping ahead a little.

With the lofty ambition 'to create the best dram in the valley', William Grant himself began distilling in 1886. He, his wife and his many children built the Glenfiddich distillery by hand; yes, by hand, in the middle of a harsh Speyside winter, with the first new make running off the stills on the crisp Christmas Day of 1887. The whole distillery was built for £800, or £40,000 in today's money. Considering the Glenfiddich brand sells limited-edition bottles of whisky for close to the latter figure, that's pretty incredible, especially as around 20 per cent of that was spent on stills bought second-hand from the Cardhu distillery.

When Pattison, the largest producer of blended Scotch whisky at the time, went bankrupt and ceased trading in 1898, the enterprising William Grant jumped at the opportunity to launch Grant's as a blended Scotch of his own. Now, more than 125 years later, Grant's is the third largest Scotch brand by volume sales in the world, shipping over 4 million cases of the product to 180 countries. Incredible. And testament to the benefit of putting everything you have behind striving towards a big ambition.

William Grant, his wife and his many children built the Glenfiddich distillery by hand; yes, by hand, in the middle of a harsh Speyside winter, with the first new make running off the stills on the crisp Christmas Day

Situated in a picturesque valley in Dufftown, Speyside, Glenfiddich, which means 'Valley of the Deer' in Gaelic, is an architecturally beautiful distillery. The building itself is nicely designed to immerse visitors in their story, whilst enjoying time in a scenic part of the world, not to mention a lovely restaurant where you can dram and feast between touring the distillery and buying whisky.

Fast forward to 1963, the year that heralded the creation of Lamborghini, Doctor Who, the humble PC mouse, The Beatles explosion, and elsewhere, Martin Luther King famously had a dream. Whilst all this was happening, Glenfiddich were quietly becoming one of the first whisky producers to commercialise the sale of single malt and push it as a premium product. This is something other producers subsequently did in order to ditch a load of excessive stock not required for their own or clients' blends at the time.

Unfortunately, William Grant & Sons were actually quite cash strapped whilst the Girvan grain distillery was being built, so the solution

Left to right: The original family crest; The lovely setting in which Glenfiddich's spirit is produced; fantastic visitor centre too, well worth a visit for a tour and a traditional lunch; Ah Warehouse No. 1, what marvellous whiskies lie in wait behind this heavy-duty door.

of selling Glenfiddich as an export product to England to raise funds was born; this was the first time single malt was marketed and promoted outside of Scotland. For context, prior to this single malt and single cask whiskies were only really available if you worked at or lived near to a distillery; they were never sold, as blends were king.

Mark Thomson, UK brand ambassador for Glenfiddich, explained further: 'You could, of course, get single malt in America at the time, but mostly if you were travelling abroad or knew someone who was. It was more the fact that you couldn't walk into a shop or bar and ask for one – nobody would know what you were talking about. They did by 1964 though.'

Nowadays, the distillery sports thirty-one stills, all designed and built to the exact same spec as the first two, with a production run of around 10 million litres of spirit per annum. Expansion plans have been submitted and approved to increase output even more by 2017. Dramtastic.

THE BOTTLE ITSELF IS ALSO UNIQUE…

These bottles were first introduced in November 1956 for the Grant's brand and later for Glenfiddich in 1961, under the watchful eye of Glenfiddich legend Charlie Grant Gordon, who we will get to know a bit better soon.

The bottle has been designed based on a sketch of a rounded triangular bottle, the 'tround', supposedly based on three core components of whisky creation – barley, water and air. It was drawn by graphic designer Hans Schleger, on to a napkin over lunch – considered a move of marketing genius – and has made Glenfiddich one of the most recognisable brands around today. As well as the tround bottles, Glenfiddich also prominently feature their twelve-point stag insignia, a marque of the brand as iconic as the bottle shape.

It was at Glenfiddich that I experienced something that has stuck with me and is often used as an analogy for why the whisky industry is amongst the best in the world.

Nothing typifies the 'all in it together'

Left: My first Glenfiddich range tasting included the Glenfiddich 40 Year Old, and the Glenfiddich 50 Year Old expressions; not a bad introduction to the brand eh?

Right: Whenever I see a 'hand fill' bottle available at a distillery, I have to buy it; rare, a reward for making the trip to the spiritual home of any whisky brand.

The bottle has been designed based on a sketch of a rounded triangular bottle, the 'tround', supposedly based on the three ingredients of whisky – barley, water and air

ethos of the whisky industry than the small town named Dufftown. The first time I visited Glenfiddich one of their most passionate brand ambassadors at the time answered my question about how competitive distilleries are between each other by sending me to the chippy.

Seriously.

I duly walked up the road, confused, having just enjoyed an immense three-course meal with him, and entered the chippy to find nine men and women in a line. Nothing remarkable, you might think, but each one of them was sporting a different brand's polo shirt, identifying the distillery they worked at, whether it be Glenfiddich, The Balvenie, Chivas or The Macallan. The area is home to so many distilleries that such uniforms are necessary. But even more surprising than the rainbow of colours in this takeaway was the fact that all of the people wearing these shirts were laughing and joking together, even brainstorming ideas as best mates would. This may sound like an obvious statement, but that just does not happen in other industries: Procter & Gamble folk fraternising with GlaxoSmithKline folk and helping them out with brand ideas? Pepsi and Coca-Cola trading syrup and distribution ideas? Not a chance.

KEEPING IT IN THE FAMILY

One thing I've not mentioned yet in relation to Glenfiddich is family.

'We stand on the shoulders of those who have gone before...and those to come will stand on ours'

Sandy Grant Gordon, ex-chairman of William Grant & Sons

Not only is this one of my favourite quotes about the William Grant & Sons business, demonstrating how it nods to the past and the future, it also typifies their entire business ethos: forward looking whilst respecting what has gone on before.

Family is huge in the world of Glenfiddich; it is currently on its sixth generation of family ownership, with an unbroken bloodline that link's today's decedents to William Grant himself. Oftentimes, family businesses get a bit of a bad rep for not being bold enough to go global, as every member of the family is always intrinsically at risk if things go south, but William Grant & Sons is completely different: family defines and guides them.

There is a lovely internal rule that no family member automatically joins the board or gets a plum job in head office. Each must leave the company, train in another industry to gain real world experience, and then return with new skills to help take the company forward; a pretty good policy in my eyes. All members of the family must also have a working knowledge of every aspect of the distillery through spending time in each role. No one is there by default; if anything the interview process is more rigorous for them being related to one another.

Being independently owned to this day is a massive deal; it has allowed the company to be bold and do new things. From opening the very first distillery visitor centre in the industry at Glenfiddich, they were also the first Scotch to export internationally (well, to Blackburn, England). They also launched the Girvan Single Grain range that kick-started an arms race in the grain whisky market between themselves, Diageo and other players. Throughout it all though, they have respected the traditions of the whisky process whilst tweaking for efficiency and researching the effects of different woods on maturation amongst many, many more interesting innovations over the years. They even bought all the valleys and hills around their water source in order to protect their water supply, the Robbie Dhu spring.

It also allows the company to plan for the long-term, without being accountable to shareholders for short-term gains or losses, or to have to answer to anyone about strategic moves that may seem maverick to the outside world.

Above: One of the mash tuns at the Glenfiddich distillery.

Right: Some of the most picturesque stills in Scotland are at the Glenfiddich distillery.

Far right: The wooden washbacks at the Glenfiddich distillery.

And boy has the brand had its fair share of mavericks over the years. Allow me to talk about just one in detail: Charlie Grant Gordon.

'I'm not short of a bob or two, not today definitely, but I [am building this for] a hundred years time'

Charlie Grant Gordon, at the age of 86

Born in 1927, Charlie was the traveller of the family, and an all-round eccentric. He had a company yacht and traversed the globe connecting with key trade customers, educating consumers, sharing knowledge and spreading the word of Scotch, single malt and Glenfiddich to the world. I would have loved to have been in the meeting when the company yacht was signed off.

These oceanic journeys are not what we know of travel today, with a plethora of airlines, budget or otherwise, getting us to every part of the known world. These were epic journeys of luck, fortune and endeavour that grew a brand, a category and a legend. In fact, Charlie was the chap who managed to introduce Scotch to nearly every continent, including North America.

From an early age Charlie knew he wanted to be a distiller; he was a student of the art of distilling both from an education and family standpoint. Sadly, though, he was unable to get into the family business at eighteen as hoped and planned; instead he was called up to the Royal Navy to help the Allies win the Second World War. Upon his return, Charlie studied for an accountancy degree at Glasgow University before going back to the family firm to become a crucial cog in the William Grant & Sons machine.

Two stories I love about Charlie...

First, a few decades ago, one of the senior production chaps saw fit to experiment with enlarging the bore holes used to fill casks; he was on a mission in order to achieve 7 per cent

additional efficiency. Charlie strolled in and asked why not increase the size of the bore holes even more, eventually increasing filling efficiency by 22 per cent. I love this constant pursuit to achieve more.

Secondly, legend has it, whilst Charlie was hosting a major distributor on his yacht, he was asked by the customer about why he had to implement the recent increase in the trade cost of Glenfiddich. Silence fell over the group for about four minutes, apparently becoming so awkward that people started admiring the boat's paintwork, before Charlie stood up, poured the client and himself a dram of Glenfiddich from his personal collection and said, 'Well, if I didn't raise the price, how the hell could I afford this yacht?' Everyone laughed, the tension was diffused and good fun ensued. What a guy.

Charlie was also responsible for the building of the Girvan grain distillery in the 1960s. Whilst construction was taking place, he would cycle round the huge site shouting orders and 'motivation' in order to encourage workers to get on with the build. The workers clearly had a sense of humour, or maybe they had balls of steel, because nine months after the build and the cycling began they welded Charlie's bicycle to the cooling towers. It remains there today. Something tells me he would have taken it in good humour.

Below: The statement-making bar at the Glenfiddich distillery.

Right: A subtle stag emblem atop a weather vane sits proudly on a pagoda warehouse.

Why I chose this chapter's suggested whisky

Glenfiddich 18 was an elusive whisky for me for a number of years; I had either enjoyed it at various whisky events or had travelled with a few miniatures of it in case the local whisky bars left me uninspired. For years I described it as 'my favourite whisky I have never owned' and had no idea why I did not just buy a bottle as it retails for around £65. Anyway, I bought one and loved it.

Glenfiddich is a great example of what a Speyside whisky should be, beautiful in its composition and with the soft, fruity yet meaty flavour profile you would expect from a whisky aged in both Oloroso sherry and bourbon casks.

CHAPTER THIRTEEN

HIGHLAND PARK

Suggested whisky:

Highland Park 18

A bit of an elusive whisky over the years for me, but in recent times, through tastings and distillery visits, I have been gratefully inducted into one of the most interesting distillery heritage stories I have heard.

Orkney itself, the brand's home, was once part of Norway, hence the Scandinavian references in both design and naming of their various whiskies. The industry's favourite whisky satirical publication, The Whisky Sponge, once stated that most Nordic mythology is in fact based on the Highland Park range. And why not.

Interestingly enough it turns out that Orcadians consider themselves more Danish than Scottish in mindset. Orkney is home to the most northerly cathedral in the UK, and for over a century Highland Park itself has been the most northerly distillery in the UK, at time of going to press…by just a few metres, until the new Shetland distillery turns on its stills in the near future.

One of their brand ambassadors once said to me:

'If you scratch the surface of Orkney, it bleeds archaeology'

And bleed archaeology it does, along with myth and mystery. Amongst local stories lies talk of Patrick Stewart, 2nd Earl of Orkney, known locally as 'Black Pat', a fierce man, who truly ruled Orkney and Shetland with an iron fist (and was ultimately executed for treason).

'If you scratch the surface of Orkney, it bleeds archaeology'

Orkney is a breeding ground for stories. The place's inscrutable nature is perhaps best demonstrated by its complete lack of trees; the sharp winds are simply too brutal for them to grow. Tales of Viking heritage and anecdotes about how the island, city and Highland Park distillery have evolved over the years, decades and centuries, are all told through intriguing myths, legends and tales of tradition.

What strikes me most about this brand is something that sets Highland Park apart from other brands, and that is the sheer number of immersive stories that exist about the distillery and sounding location. I'd hedge a bet this charismatic heritage might play a part in the prominence of the brand, which has enjoyed a meteoric rise in the last decade or so. And it is these stories which influence the Highland Park releases, not only their names but their flavour profile.

Take one of the components of its much enjoyed and collected Valhalla Collection, Thor, for example. The liquid does exactly as you would expect from the name: it conveys power and packs a punch without being overstated about it all.

I'm a big fan of Edrington. I like how the company rewards its staff, how passionate its staff are and also how they all work together for a higher cause – to not only grow brands to their

bottom line but to also inspire whisky drinkers with special whisky releases laden with rich, evocative stories. Highland Park is no different; there is a genuine pride about the distillery staff, and a buzz around each release amongst them.

This is not a distillery that churns out spirit for the sake of it: Highland Park releases special products at just the right time. The people behind the process are not only excited about the fruits of their labour making it to market, but they agonise over how those will be received by writers, consumers, collectors, whisky lovers and the wider spectrum of Highland Park considerers. The people behind Highland Park care; it's instinct.

The liquid does exactly as you would expect from the name: it conveys power and packs a punch without being overstated about it all

ALL ABOUT PROVENANCE

The barley Highland Park uses, called Concerto, comes from the mainland, but for the past few years, they have been cultivating a local strain of barley called Tartan that is grown on the island that will be hand malted and eventually appear in Highland Park bottlings. I love a distillery with malting floors, and it is getting rarer to see such a sight, but Highland Park has three that are worked hard, smell amazing and…are curiously Y-shaped.

Left to right: The beginnings of the whisky making process; the malting rooms at Highland Park; fuel for the kiln; the kiln red hot for drying the barley.

Orkney peat is unique to honey heather moorland, hence that sweet yet slightly smoky taste profile unheard of anywhere else

FOR PEAT'S SAKE

Orkney peat is unique to honey heather moorland, hence that sweet yet slightly smoky taste profile unheard of anywhere else.

The peat actually forms in three layers:

1. Top layers have the roots from the heather, which give us the sweet notes
2. Second layer gives the aromatic notes
3. The final layers are pretty solid, very few roots and add the hint of smokiness

The heather moorland owned by Highland Park spans 1,000 acres and when I asked how long it would take to run out of peat, I was firmly told: 'We have been distilling since 1798 and are not even halfway through the first 250 acres, so we will be okay for a while.' Lots of limited editions to come, then!

THINKING ABOUT THE BRAND

Ancient kings. Norse mythology. Tribal symbolism. Dark and mysterious packaging. These are just a few of the things that come to mind when I think about the Highland Park brand.

An old intern of mine used to tell me how much his grandad enjoyed Highland Park whisky. I vaguely remember seeing the old brand years ago, but aside from that I had to discover, or rather rediscover, the brand a couple of years ago in order to fully understand it.

With packaging that creates what we in the design world refer to as 'great shelf blocking' – a visual device to grab the attention of shoppers by literally blocking shelves with your brand colours, symbols and messages – Highland Park has seen a remarkable revival in recent years.

Like many single malts that were formerly blend fodder, Highland Park used to be viewed as a 'whisky my dad drinks', but what a lot of people don't know is that its 25 Year Old was the first whisky in the world to score a perfect 100 points in the International Spirits Competition.

Nowadays, Highland Park has a cult following akin to Ardbeg's, as well as being popular in the mainstream with some incredible super premium releases that are held in as high regard as their mainline 12 and 18 Year Olds.

There's a superb tale of a bunch of Scandinavians coming over to Orkney for a visit,

Above: The tasting bar at the Highland Park distillery.

Left: Old stencils used to brand and label casks.

Like many single malts that were formerly blend fodder, Highland Park used to be viewed as a 'whisky my dad drinks'

a tour, a tasting, the works, and then buying so much whisky in the distillery shop that their plane literally could not take off. No word of a lie.

The 18 Year Old is one of my most savoured whiskies, and the mysterious, almost dark visual style of the latest pack design is evocative of immense backstories, both mythological and evolutionary. That's what makes this brand so interesting: the packaging links so well to the island and its surroundings. The stories that have been passed through generations spanning centuries live through product names, pack designs and branded experiences that are so carefully crafted that you would not believe.

Ever wondered why Highland Park Odin tastes why it does? Or why Freya was different to Odin, or why each release adds another strand to the flavour profile of this great brand? The answer is simple: you are appreciating them in different ways, as the stories have been crafted in such a way that they take the expected distillery heritage and soak it in tales of the past that anyone can get lost in.

Graphically, the design system is a lot better than it used to be. As I mentioned above, the 'menacing black' stands out, especially with silver embossing (or other colours depending on the release) coupled with Viking-esque weapons, all of which make it all just 'feel' right.

And the fantastic Highland Park Dark Origins release? How apt a name – this island, this brand and this packaging tells us about varying degrees of dark origins. Now go forth and see what you get differently from each release.

Why I chose this chapter's suggested whisky

Similar to a few other suggested whiskies, I first tried Highland Park 18 at the distillery where my host, the immensely passionate and knowledgeable Pat, described the 18 Year Old as 'Orkney in a glass'. Even from my limited time on Orkney, I could tell she was not wrong.

It is one to savour, not to overthink. For me, I get smoke, salt, maritime and heather honey filling the nose followed by a really enjoyable mouthfeel with a well-rounded palate that always makes me long for more.

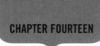
ABERLOUR

Suggested whisky:

Aberlour 18 Year Old

Dating back to 1826, and situated right in the heart of Speyside, Aberlour is a Gaelic word meaning 'mouth of the chattering burn'.

Nowadays, Aberlour is owned by Pernod Ricard's Chivas Brothers subsidiary, but this was not always the case, as you shall soon find out. Despite officially opening in 1826, and being owned by James Grant, a fire destroyed most of the distillery in 1878. Local rich fella James Fleming was responsible for resurrecting the distillery and rebuilding most of what we now know as the Aberlour distillery in 1879, slightly away from the original site in order to make use of the local water source.

Situated a stone's throw from the River Spey,

in picturesque Speyside, Aberlour is a lovely distillery that produces around 4 million litres of spirit a year and delivers an experience that is immersive, has stunning tasting rooms and a lovely tour that showcases the best of traditional whisky.

I actually use Aberlour's 10 Year Old entry-level expression in a lot of my tastings as it provides such a fantastic flavour and introduction to sherry-matured whisky, for a relatively small amount of money. It also happens to have won a bunch of awards and has contributed handsomely to Aberlour being one of the top-selling Scotch single malts in the world, and the top one in France.

I actually use Aberlour's 10 Year Old entry-level expression in a lot of my tastings as it provides such a fantastic flavour and introduction to sherry-matured whisky

AN EXCLUSIVE INVITATION

Midway through 2016, I was asked to visit the distillery to become one of just a handful of people inducted into the Aberlour A'bunadh Collective: an exclusive, invitation-only group made up of like-minded whisky experts who share Aberlour's passion for artisanal, small batch single malt Scotch whisky.

Such a kind description, but one that summed up a superb group of people including a good whisky friend of mine and great guy, Matt Chambers of WhiskyForEveryone, and Mr Lyan (real name Ryan Chetiyawardana) of Dandelyan,

White Lyan and mixology competition fame, who describes himself quite accurately as one of the 'most studious of bartending gentlemen'; a thoroughly nice chap he is too.

In the words of Chivas Brothers on the official invite:

'The Aberlour A'bunadh Collective has been set up to provide Aberlour's biggest supporters with a series of insights into the world of single malt to continue the Aberlour legend. As a respected expert in the field, we would like to invite you to join Aberlour A'bunadh Collective'

ABERLOUR
A'BUNADH COLLECTIVE
2016

DANIEL SHEN
DAWN DAVIES
GREG DILLON
IAN WISNIEWSKI
MATT CHAMBERS
OTTO FLAT
PÉRIGO LEGASSE
RACHEL McCORMACK
RYAN CHETIYAWARDANA
SEAN KENYON

Above: The Inaugural
A'bunadh Collective.

Left: Matt Chambers
of WhiskyForEveryone,
and Mr Lyan (real name
Ryan Chetiyawardana) of
Dandelyan, White Lyan and
mixology competition fame.

Far left: A line up of liquid
gold.

My creation was deemed to be 'big and bold, just like [you]' by the chair of the Aberlour A'bunadh Collective

You simply don't turn down an invitation like that, even if the event itself comes a day after a particularly brutal stag do.

The get-together, held at the Aberlour distillery up in Speyside, was absolutely superb and a solid reinforcement of the craft and traditional nature of Aberlour, and especially Aberlour A'bunadh. One of my highlights from the trip was when each of us spent the afternoon blending our own Aberlour A'bunadh from a set of single-cask samples; it was incredible, especially seeing how many different expressions can be created from the same few input whiskies.

My creation was deemed to be 'big and bold, just like [you]' by the chair of the Aberlour A'bunadh Collective. He had a point: I bottled my 200ml, wrote the label that read 'Limited Edition 1 of 1' and casually nosed the creations of a couple of the other guests. We also had a warehouse tasting in the warehouse where a cask end with all our names etched on is now mounted. A true honour.

Now, as monumental as this was, this event was also the first time I have ever worn a kilt.

Naturally I was petrified of wearing the kilt incorrectly, no instructions were provided. I had to follow YouTube videos whilst I battled tartan, massive socks, impossibly long shoe laces and a sporran, which I later discovered was a perfect phone and room-key holder. Once the fear had subsided, and the kilt and full dress attire adorned, I was whisked off to the distillery for the stunning traditional Scottish dinner held in the distillery where we were treated to the full Piping of the Haggis ceremony, including the 'Address to a Haggis'.

Facing page (far left) top: Flavour notes and proportions used to work out the make up of my 1 of 1 Aberlour A'bunadh Collective single malt.

Facing page (far left) below: My effort at blending my own single malt.

Right: My first time in a kilt on my way to the Aberlour A'bunadh Collective Dinner.

The meal was amazing, theatrical and full of excitement for the brand, the different whiskies they produce and, of course, the people in the room. We then headed back to Linn House, the guesthouse we were staying in that is only open to 'VIP and VVIP' guests of Chivas Brothers' brands, to take a look at the Garden Bar whilst sampling products from across the Chivas portfolio. What a treat.

If you get to visit the distillery then please take advantage of its premium tastings. Something very special is normally whipped out, occasionally from dead distilleries, that will give you a real treat and a taste for the good stuff. You can even buy a bottle of Aberlour at cask strength that has been hand filled either that day or the day before (correct as of September 2016).

There is something special about Aberlour, I often think it is underrated, or at least not spoken about enough in whisky circles. For me, the brand's range shows what can be done with whiskies of different ages and vintages aged in sherry casks, mostly without breaking the bank.

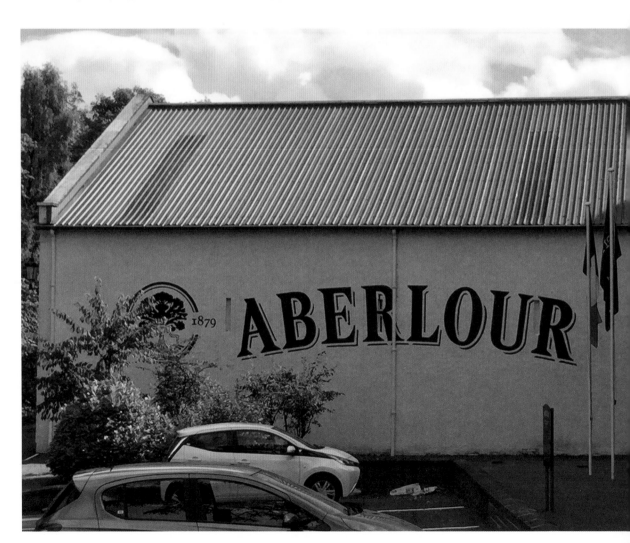

Left: The Aberlour Distillery.

Above: The samples I had available to create my special single malt from.

*If you get to visit the distillery then please take advantage
of its premium tastings. Something very special is normally
whipped out, occasionally from dead distilleries, that
will give you a real treat and a taste for the good stuff*

The Aberlour A'bunadh and the Aberlour 18 Year Old in particular are stunning, A'bunadh has a hefty ABV and is bottled in batches, but do not be put off. This is a great-value dram, matured in first-fill sherry casks, that packs a punch: a full-bodied palate, meaty, lots of dried fruits and dark Christmas fruits. Scrumptious. In case you were wondering, it is pronounced 'ah-boo-na'.

Above: The door to the legendary Warehouse No. 1 at the Aberlour Distillery.

Right: A lovely stylised cask end seen in The Craigellachie Hotel in Speyside.

Why I chose this chapter's suggested whisky

As you can probably tell, Aberlour has a very special place in my heart, and A'bunadh especially, but I thought I'd go with another product in the Aberlour stable that does not get enough credit in my opinion: the Aberlour 18 Year Old. This whisky is delicately rich with a healthy amount of spice and oodles of fresh apples and other fruits, all rounded off with a caressing sherry note that brings with it dark and dried fruits. Always a go-to favourite of mine.

CHAPTER FIFTEEN

THE DALMORE

Suggested whisky:

The Dalmore King Alexander III

The Dalmore, wow, oh wow, The Dalmore. One of the most exclusive drams you will come across, with many of their limited editions costing a comfortable four figures; other more special releases have sold at auction for over £100,000.

Why? Well, aside from being a stunning liquid, the man, nay whisky icon at the helm of the distillery and brand is none other than Richard Paterson, a fifty-year veteran of the whisky industry.

The distillery itself has one of the longest-standing stories in whisky, dating back to 1263 when Scotland was clan-based and ruled by King Alexander III who was saved from near-certain death when a stag charged straight for him, by a shout of 'Cuidich 'n' Righ', which means 'Save the King!' in Gaelic, by Colin of Kintail who subsequently killed the stag by slamming a spear straight into its forehead.

In recognition of this act of bravery and quick thinking, King Alexander III granted Colin of Kintail, Chief of the Clan Mackenzie, a healthy amount of land and, crucially, the use of the twelve-pointed stag within his clan's crest, an honour typically reserved for royalty.

Fast-forward to 1867 and, after twenty-eight years of ownership by Sir Alexander Matheson, who deliberately placed The Dalmore to the north of Speyside to differentiate his product

The distillery itself has one of the longest-standing stories in whisky, dating back to 1263 when Scotland was clan-based and ruled by King Alexander III...

1263

The Dalmore's heritage dates back to 1263, when an ancestor of the Clan Mackenzie, owners of The Dalmore distillery for over a century, saved King Alexander III from the fury of a charging stag. In recognition of this noble act the grateful King granted the Clan Mackenzie the right to use a 12-point stag, representing a 'Royal', in their coat of arms. This striking icon has since adorned each bottle of The Dalmore, symbolising The Dalmore distillery's regal legacy.

THE ART OF THE DALMORE

The Dalmore is crafted using a 150 year old artisan process passed down through the generations. Eight hand beaten copper stills of variable shape and size deliver a full flavoured and complex new spirit, which is then enriched over the years in the finest American white oak ex-bourbon casks and hand selected oloroso sherry butts. Master Distiller Richard Paterson then makes his final selection, harmonising the spirit of the chosen casks in bespoke sherry butts until he decides that the precious contents are ready for bottling.

TASTING NOTES

Crafted to honour the act of saving Scotland's King in 1263, this expression unites six specially selected casks housing spirit of perfect maturity. Whiskies matured in ex-bourbon casks, Matusalem oloroso sherry wood, Madeira barrels, Marsala casks, port pipes and Cabernet Sauvignon wine barriques are brought together in perfect harmony. Each cask gives its own flavour notes, delivering a unique complex single malt whisky revered by connoisseurs.

Aroma   Red berry fruits, fresh flowers and hints of passion fruit
Palate   Citrus zest, vanilla pod, crème caramel and crushed almonds
Finish   Sweet cinnamon, nutmeg, cloves and ginger

from the masses at the time, The Dalmore brand was under the control of the Mackenzie Brothers, who dutifully applied the Royal twelve-point stag, a symbol of their clan, to the packaging.

All was well with production for the next half century until the First World War brought in the Navy who, for three years, occupied the distillery, leaving a right mess that took a further two years to fix after their departure.

Nowadays, the distillery is owned by Emperador, who by all accounts is investing heavily and working to build the brand throughout the world.

Above: The mighty The Dalmore King Alexander III.

IN THE PRESENCE A LEGEND AND THE NOSE EXTRAORDINAIRE

In early 2016, I was invited up to The Dalmore distillery to get immersed in the brand, the place and attend a private whisky tasting with Richard Paterson. Can you guess how excited I was? I'm sure regular GreatDrams readers and followers on social media will know how much I love my job and how grateful I am to be in a position where I get to experience the best of the whisky industry. This whisky tasting was no exception, and in reality was catapulted right up to be one of the top experiences I've had in the whisky industry: two days of his time, his conversation, his wit, his knowledge, his insistence on how many Wednesdays it has rained throughout the history of whisky, his passion, his undeniable likability and, of course, his whisky. One of only a couple of times I have actually felt like a bit of a groupie in the industry, I was excited throughout. It would be tough for anyone not to be, and if they said they were not, they had just lied to you.

Of course, I was there to learn about more than how charming Richard is, but he embodies what it means to be not only a Master Distiller but also a Master of Ceremonies and Brand Ambassador: the charisma, the agonising over getting things right and ensuring people all over the world enjoy great whisky in interesting and respectful ways is amazing. Only a few others in the industry have that prowess and stature when they walk into a room, but many more should. He even posed for a selfie during my tourist moment before our tasting (and then again a few months later at the launch of his new release, The Dalmore Quintessence).

Right: Myself with one of the true characters of whisky; Richard Paterson.

Below: The range of whiskies we sampled that night — love their packaging.

The seven of us in attendance did the distillery tour, walked around taking photos and finished by sampling a beautiful expression of The Dalmore, then we were ushered upstairs to the whisky-tasting room. This place is the epicentre of the brand, the pinnacle of The Dalmore experience. Akin to how much the brand is integrated into the tasting rooms of the Glenturret distillery, no detail is left to chance.

We sat, we waited, we eyed up the bottles at one end of the room and the seven copita glasses in front of us, each containing a hearty measure for us to nose, sample, discuss and enjoy. After an introduction and recap of various discussion points we had been over through the day about casks, the distillery, spirit style and whatnot we got started with The Dalmore new make at a warming 68% ABV.

'Now, none of this diving straight into the whisky nonsense,' Richard proclaimed with a knowing smile. 'Roll the glass from one nostril to the other and back again as you nose, get stuck in, but if your eyes go weird you are nosing too aggressively.' I had never heard of aggressive nosing, but dutifully complied and got stuck in. A really nice new make, cotton notes, a bit of baby sick (ugh) but it was deep, thick and heavy.

When sampling The Dalmore 12 Year Old, Richard introduced the whisky by explaining that 'chocolate orange notes are our house style, the base spirit should evoke this along with a soft, fruity, vanilla undertone'. He went on to tell us how he loved international guests as it meant he got to understand more global opinions and the differences between peoples' perceptions, as well as how others describe certain things. The caveat with that this not being completely the case for the English opinion… as I looked at him in disbelief he gave my beard a little rub and all was well again.

The nose gave me dark fruit, orange, Christmas cake and old English marmalade, sweet but with depth. The palate opened up to reveal spices, more orange and a medium length finish. All in all a nice whisky, one I could spend a lot of time with, but my favourite in the range would come a little later.

We then tried The Dalmore 18 Year Old. Game on.

'This one is all about marmalade, that is what you should and will be getting,' proclaimed Richard. 'This has spent fourteen years in American white oak and four years, YEARS, in sherry casks as an elongated finish.'

The nose was thick, so thick, incredible sherry notes and that orange character he spoke about. The palate was a masterclass in flavours, one of the most flavoursome whiskies I've enjoyed in a long while. There was mint, marmalade, rich fruits, chocolate, hints of balsamic, liquorice, all wrapped in an earthy surround. The finish was spicy and warm with sherry notes kicking in again. Holy wow, that was incredible, truly amazing and great value in my opinion when you put it side by side against other 18 Year Old whiskies.

We then tried what ultimately became the recommended dram for this chapter, The Dalmore King Alexander III, but more on that a little later.

The final pre-dinner dram was of course The Dalmore 25 Year Old: 'Now the thing to understand here is that only 1 per cent, yes 1 per cent of this whisky is twenty-five years old. Seventy per cent of it is twenty-eight years old and 29 per cent of it is thirty-three years old, that's just how we do things around here.'

Richard explained how this dram was strongly influenced by Cubism and Paul Cezanne in particular in the way it could bring a subject to life and give it depth that alluded to 3D structures. The whisky itself is mostly matured in American white oak, then Palomino Fino sherry for two years and finally Tawny Port casks for eighteen months. Only 3,000 bottles are released every year. The nose was, as you might expect by now, exceptional: fresh apples, soft caramels. The palate gave off such a silky yet rich flavour you could be forgiven for falling in love with it instantly. It was elegant, luxurious, immense.

A FAMILY OF WHISKIES

Something I hope you will agree with me on when you sample The Dalmore range is how consistent the style is across each and every expression; they conform to base notes that Richard looks for, no compromising, no rogue elements, just a great family of whiskies.

Separately, given many of The Dalmore releases do not have age statements, I asked Richard for his view on the No Age Statement subject that gets so many column inches in the whisky press. He passionately answered my question thus: 'None of my counterparts would ever release anything unless it was up to a very high standard; it just won't happen, their reputation is always on the line. It takes time to bring whisky together in loving union but age is not the most important thing.'

For example: The Dalmore's 25 Year Old single malt, a divine whisky, has only 1 per cent 25 Year Old whisky in there; the rest is made up of much more aged liquids. You don't get to know the full composition unless you ask a few questions and have access to certain people. Age is clearly important for this release as it is one of their marque expressions, but the number effectively comes second to the liquid quality itself.

You will have read at the beginning of this book that I am passionately behind the expressive nature of creating whiskies that are not bound by age but by flavour profile that brings distillery stories to life, so I won't go in to it again.

Another fascinating experience with The Dalmore I want to tell you about is when, at the launch of The Dalmore Quintessence, I was introduced to a concept that would make me think more about how I sample whisky for evermore.

Above: An old delivery truck for The Dalmore.

Below: The bottle factory – KEEP CLEAR!

The launch itself was centred around mindfulness: taking the time to truly appreciate every detail, nuance, aroma, feeling and flavour without rushing or shortcutting the overall experience. We were introduced to the concept by using a humble raisin as an example of how something so small and otherwise unimposing can have a profound affect on the understanding of flavour.

We then applied the same technique of calming ourselves, spending time understanding our breathing, taking a considered look at the whisky's colour, examining the nose, the sensation of the liquid on our lips, then our tongues, then under our tongues, then finally when swallowing The Dalmore Quintessence.

It was a fascinating example of slowing things down, not rushing through the sampling of a new liquor, and enjoying every element of the whisky, and food, experience. This experience also allowed for a greater number of flavour notes to be identified than usual on the first pass of whisky tasting.

By approaching whisky in this way, and noting that I, like many in attendance who regularly review and analyse their whisky do this without realising there is a real science behind it, I was able to pull apart the whisky in much more depth, and enjoyed the process...although it would slow things down if this was done for every single whisky we all tried.

My notes read thus:

The colour was deep, burning gold wrapped in a light red hue. The nose brought about a plethora of wine and sweetness rounded off with a distinct burnt sugar note with hints of vanilla, dark fruits, juicy peaches and the classic chunky marmalade character of The Dalmore distillery's signature style. On the palate silky caramel notes shone through as the liquid turned velvety and creamy with marzipan notes, only a light alcohol feeling and a chocolate orange character developed before being replaced by white peppers and spice.

Above: A cask waiting outside the distillery being subjected to the weather.

Right: An ancient stone crest in the grounds of the distillery.

Above: One of the most luxurious whisky tasting flights I've had the privilege to be a part of.

Why I chose this chapter's suggested whisky

As promised, here is just a couple of reasons I chose The Dalmore King Alexander III as my whisky of choice for this chapter.

The Dalmore King Alexander III is the only six-finish single malt in the world and it is an absolute belter of a dram. 'What are the six casks used?' I hear you cry… Madeira, sherry, wine, Marsala, small-batch bourbon and port pipes – an epic 'assemblage' of flavour and skill to weave these notes together. The nose is all about marzipan and plums, orange here and there, but the palate is where it all kicks off: tannins, salt, apples, chocolate, fresh oranges and many more. A true cacophony of flavours.

The finish lingers. This is another highly sippable dram, and one Richard refers to as 'a highly conversational whisky'…it also happens to be his favourite recreational whisky whilst travelling.

IT'S GREAT DRAMS WHISKY TASTING TIME

Think about the nose and palate…
What notes are you getting? Is it…
Sweet? Sour? Smoky? Spicy?
Summer fruits? Winter fruits?
Oakiness? All of these?
None of these?

Try to decode what your nose and palate
are telling you – everyone's experience
with whisky is personal and can
vary so feel free to explore and
understand your senses…

Your notes

Remember to tell me how you get on with each whisky from the book on
Twitter, Facebook and Instagram: #GreatDramsOfScotland

 /GreatDrams  @GreatDrams  greatdramsgreg

THE UNDISCOVERED

CHAPTER SIXTEEN

CRAIGELLACHIE

Suggested whisky:

Craigellachie 23 (distillery bottling)

Craigellachie is a distillery no one outside of the profession gets to see, but it is one that has a fantastic story behind it and has released some absolutely superb products for us all to enjoy.

Nowadays Craigellachie is owned by Bacardi as part of their subsidiary, John Dewar & Sons. The range comprises single malts from distilleries that traditionally only made whisky for blend fodder: Craigellachie, The Deveron, Aultmore, Royal Brackla and Aberfeldy.

Aside from the recent distillery releases of 13, 17, 19, 23 and the 31 travel retail exclusive, you and most other whisky drinkers will only have experienced the produce from this workhorse of a distillery in single-cask releases from independent bottlers. The reason is that the bulk of its production would have historically gone into the White Horse blend, and in more recent times into the blends owned by Bacardi.

The distillery itself dates back to 1891 when whisky royalty Alexander Edward, who owned the Benrinnes distillery, and Sir Peter Mackie, who had a history of making successful whisky brands and operating multiple distilleries, formed a formidable partnership. Mackie already owned the Lagavulin distillery on Islay and had created the White Horse blend that meant Craigellachie was able to ride the peaks and troughs of the whisky industry. Over the next 125 years it endured the same market ups and downs as their competitors, such as the infamous Patterson Crisis when many distilleries went to the wall, but it managed to ride it and succeed where others failed.

Craigellachie is a distillery no one outside of the profession gets to see, but it is one that has a fantastic story behind it and has released some absolutely superb products for us all to enjoy

Mackie also believed in maintaining good health and insisted that his employees were fed properly through what their archives describe as 'BBM – blood, bone and meal'. I have no idea what was contained in such a meal, but it was fed to the employees on site every day.

The genius of Edward and Mackie's partnership was what many brands strive for today in whisky: an answer to different whisky taste preferences with their different distillery products, from Benrinnes and Craigellachie to Lagavulin, a flavour spectrum spanning smooth to smoky.

Over the years Craigellachie has had the fortune to have its original equipment maintained incredibly well, meaning it is now one of few distilleries to use oil to fire its stills and still worm tubs for the cooling of the spirit. In case you haven't come across these rare tanks before, worm tubs comprise copper tubes that are narrower at the end than at the beginning and which sit in cold-water tanks. In modern or modernised distilleries worm tubs would have been replaced by or fitted with condensers instead. The result? A spirit they refer to as having 'a distinctive, meaty character', and I can testify that this whisky is somewhat heavier than others I have tasted and is all the better for it: the

Craigellachie 23, which is the suggested whisky for this chapter, is simply sublime.

As well as having ancient equipment, the distillery has a very interesting cat story.

Most distilleries have cats; they are dedicated 'mousers'. The Guinness World Record-holding feline, Towser of the Glenturret Distillery, averaged three mouse kills a day during her life, which equated to around 28,899 kills. Craigellachie too had a famous cat, who features on their current packaging, but this cat performed a different role: it hated the smell of spirit vapour so would dart out of the still house whenever that vapour was present, thus alerting the stillmen that it was time to turn the steam off.

From a design perspective I love the company's bottle and secondary pack designs. I might be a touch biased as I know the chaps who designed them, but in my honest opinion they are amongst the best out there for raw authenticity, grit and storytelling. The bottles and tubes do not have the polished luxury of The Macallan, sure, but they all exude a realism that evokes the character of not only the whisky itself, but the terroir in which it has lived for years until bottling.

...it is now one of few distilleries to use oil to fire its stills and still worm tubs for the cooling of the spirit

Why I chose this chapter's suggested whisky

Craigellachie 23 is my wife Kirsty's favourite whisky. So much so I have had to hide the bottle to make sure it lasts! Really heavy on the sherry notes, this is a knockout whisky. Sweet, sulphur, thick, raw, rounded…there are so many words to describe this one. Kirsty tells me that it is her favourite because of the 'huge sherry influence, the way the whisky consumes the mouth and just tastes amazing.'

From my standpoint, I also like how it feels old school, likely due to those worm tubs used in the production, and the sulphur note that I often do not like about other whiskies just seems to work. A true knockout.

CHAPTER SEVENTEEN

GLENGLASSAUGH

Suggested whisky:

Glenglassaugh Torfa

In his 1887 tome The Whisky Distilleries of the United Kingdom, Alfred Barnard once described this distillery as 'too well known to need any praise'. Lofty praise indeed from the first person on record to have crossed the threshold of every distillery in the United Kingdom at the time. I did not recognise the bottle of Glenglassaugh Revival when presented with it a few Christmases ago by my brother-in-law, so it sat on my shelf for about three years, waiting to be devoured. Odd as it may sound, I'm glad I didn't crack it open until after I'd visited the Glenglassaugh distillery; a drink means so much more when you know the journey the distillery and brand have been on.

The history of this distillery is relatively turbulent, with a curious mix of the architecture of two different centuries occupying the site. Glenglassaugh's story starts in 1874 when Colonel James Moir commissioned the distillery to be built at a cost of £10,000, or £700,000 in today's money, with the first spirit running from the still in April 1875. Moir operated it for just under two decades until the distillery was bought by Highland Distillers in 1892. Sadly, unlike Craigellachie, Glenglassaugh did not survive the Patterson crash, likely due to it being a unique whisky that stood too tall against other component whiskies in the various blends it was present in. The distillery was subsequently

Alfred Barnard once described this distillery as
'too well known to need any praise'

mothballed between 1907 and 1960.

Between 1959 and 1960 the distillery was refurbished, and practically rebuilt in order to distil again after the hiatus. This renaissance was short-lived, however; in 1986 the distillery was closed yet again as it was not seen as economically viable to operate a distillery in such a far-flung location.

Glenglassaugh reopened in 2008 and was subsequently bought by the Scaent Group, a Russian-backed consortium, for around £5 million. In 2013 the distillery was added to the expanding BenRiach stable of Scotch distilleries, and in 2016 was bought by Brown-Forman as part of their acquisition of The BenRiach Distillery Company, which included GlenDronach, BenRiach and Glenglassaugh, for £285 million.

On my first visit to the distillery, situated next to the sea and a lovely beach and whose name means 'valley of the green fields', I realised I could not have found a more undiscovered gem. My Instagram post immediately after visiting read: 'possibly the best distillery I've been to', and I stand by it still.

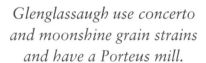

*Glenglassaugh use concerto
and moonshine grain strains
and have a Porteus mill.*

AN IMPRESSIVE VISIT
TO A HIDDEN GEM

Often you get a really good feeling about a place when you are there and in the moment, but a few hours later you dissect the experience properly and realise that maybe your initial impression of the place no longer rings true. However, my first impression of Glenglassaugh has stayed with me to this day.

It all started without much funfair. We had arrived at the Glenglassaugh distillery early so we could spend time walking along the beach, dipping our hands in the sea (a tradition started by my father-in-law when meeting a new sea on his travels around the world) and climbing up a hill with a view of the bay on which the distillery is crowned.

As I entered the visitor centre, I spotted a cask I would later revisit to bottle my own 8 Year Old Glenglassaugh, matured in a first-fill sherry cask.

Facing page (far left): A racked warehouse full of whisky waiting to be blended.

Facing page: The gorgeous views from the bay down the road from Glenglassaugh's distillery.

Below: A firmly sealed barrel.

Our first stop was the maltings, dating back to around 1922, which are no longer in use but are retained and maintained in all their lovely antiquarian glory.

Glenglassaugh use concerto and moonshine grain strains and have a Porteus mill. Although built in the 1930s, the malt mill itself was only installed in 1959 during the refurb. The whole distillery is operated by cogs and turns with only one switch panel that looks like something out of Lost (google it).

Three stillmen, working in shifts, operate the stills. Four wooden and two steel washbacks lurk in the corner, with the wooden ones dating back to 1875! All in all, the distillery produces approximately 1 million litres of spirit per year.

The distillery sits deep in the Scottish Highlands, and as we wandered through the warehouses and walked amongst sleeping casks, there were stories about each to be told. The distillery itself was on its summer hiatus when we visited, so no spirit was being produced, but you

Above: Filling my own bottle of single cask Glenglassaugh; beautiful expression.

could tell by just observing the resting machinery that this was a well-loved place; everything had its place and had been maintained impeccably.

I nosed many casks that day and saw some superb old whisky casks 'resting' through the site (some of which were dated 1963, which is coincidentally the year single malt became commercialised alongside blended Scotch). All in all there were 17,194 casks just in warehouse five when I visited…so there's plenty of stock maturing for future releases.

When I left, I was left reminiscing over a really genuine distillery experience, and yet I struggle to articulate the experience itself. For me this place needs to be visited to experience the history, the scenery, the work ethic and, of course, the spirit itself.

Why I chose this chapter's suggested whisky

Whilst visiting the distillery in late 2015 I did a range tasting, and a sample tasting a few months later. Out of both, Glenglassaugh Torfa is the whisky that really stood out for me.

Derived from the old Norse word for peat, Glenglassaugh Torfa is the first peated release, at a respectable 20PPM, from Glenglassaugh. The whisky is aged to around four or five years old and is bottled at a punchy 50% ABV having been matured in ex-bourbon casks.

On the nose you'll get sweet peat, reminiscent of Highland Park, and medicinal notes which feel mature despite the spirit's youth. The palate opens, offering a lot with more smoke than the nose, giving a salty yet sweet note. This dram is a series of delicious juxtapositions.

Hints of lemon and milk chocolate in the background are followed by a lingering, soothing finish that retains its smoky notes throughout. I wonder if and when there will be an aged release of the Torfa? I would definitely be interested in exploring the brand's products as and when it expands its range, as this, along with Revival, shows a ton of potential. Saying that, I have heard its ancient releases are delightful. Maybe one day...

CHAPTER EIGHTEEN

THE GLENROTHES

Suggested whisky:

The Glenrothes 1985 Vintage or The Glenrothes Sherry Cask Reserve

The Glenrothes: a brand that until recently was owned by Berry Bros. & Rudd, living in a distillery owned by Edrington (and since the time of writing this book, bought back by Edrington) – such is the weird and wonderful way of the world of whisky.

When I visited Rothes House in the autumn of 2015, it was still with its former owner. I was hosted by Ronnie Cox who still heads up heritage brands for Berry Bros. & Rudd. Ronnie walked us around and gave us a few minutes to freshen up after our travels, before sitting us down for a homemade fish pie and chatting about Scottish and distillery history.

If ever a brand had a strong character pushing it forward, that brand was The Glenrothes. Ronnie is someone so full of energy, fun, personality and great stories. When he speaks, you listen, fully engaged, as his manner is down to earth but, and I hope he does not mind me saying so, sage-like in the depth of his intimate knowledge about Berry Bros. & Rudd, just as it was of The Glenrothes when he used to host guests of the brand

Curiously, the distillery manager's house at The Glenrothes is smaller than the house given to the excise man of old; back in the day, plush accommodation was offered to keep the taxman at bay. We also walked through the cemetery with its intriguing headstone carvings dating back beyond the plague, in some cases with symbols to denote manner of death. We also learned how the Church in the Parish of Knockando actually loaned The Glenrothes the cash to finish building the distillery following the 'Big Crash' of 1878–79.

It really is a 'spiritual' place – excuse the pun – for whisky lovers, and myself specifically, as despite spending a fair amount of time in Scotland nowadays, I always get a buzz when I visit

THE GLENROTHES

SHERRY CASK RESERVE
SPEYSIDE SINGLE MALT SCOTCH WHISKY

CHARACTER: *Spicy ginger, orange-peel & sherry oak*

APPROVED: *Gordon Motion*   Malt Master

FOUNDED IN 1879 SPEYSIDE SCOTLAND

Distilled and Bottled in Scotland. Berry Bros. & Rudd Ltd, 3 St. James's Street, London
PRODUCT OF SCOTLAND

In total there are twenty washbacks at The Glenrothes, eight steel and twelve Oregon pine. All of the washbacks have a sixty-hour fermentation cycle that produces a 10% ABV wash, although it didn't taste that high in ABV when we sipped. The spirit is no longer peated at all. The casks get filled at 69.8% ABV.

Then we were taken to a warehouse to have a go at drawing whisky from various casks whilst sampling the wonders of The Glenrothes' spirit that had been filled in 2014, 2010 and 1987... and we loved every single drop.

Just next to these casks is their '$1m store' – a set of bottles containing whisky that was distilled in the sixties and seventies, bottled at 40% ABV and that will sell for around £7,500 per bottle when eventually released... We were not allowed to try these!

Then, with a great reveal, we entered a door with the letters 'I. S.' ominously placed above the entrance: The Inner Sanctum. In here we sampled the core range, dissecting the flavours and chatting about each one in depth, the shape of the bottle and more about the history of the distillery, then Ronnie, with his charismatic wit and dry humour, whipped out some very special drams indeed.

The room itself is lovely, it is exactly what I want from my office, in truth – all the furniture,

and I mean all of it, is linked to the process and to casks in some way and most has been designed and built bespoke for this special place. In the middle of the room there is a huge round table that was made in the spirit of King Arthur: round so that everyone has an equal opinion and that hierarchy is never present.

Adorning the walls are bottles from through the decades, a true celebration of the brand and a true belief in what they stand for and the quality of their product. Ever curious about a brand's bottle design, I asked about its origins and learnt that the bottle is an extension of the sample bottles of yesteryear, including the label, in order to differentiate and stand out with a modern bottle design.

Crucial to point out here that the distillery is not open to the public, only to press and trade. Sorry folks.

Another interesting fact I picked up from the knowledge fount that is Ronnie, is that most Master Blenders typically sample their whiskies at around 20% ABV to ensure it works when water/ice/mixers are added as well as when served neat at 40% ABV and above.

On with the tasting...

Facing page (far left): Some old tools of the trade sit in one of the warehouses at The Glenrothes.

Facing page: Old, and decommissioned equipment.

Below: Shhhhhh!

First up was The Glenrothes Bourbon Cask Reserve, 40%, matured exclusively in ex-bourbon casks. The nose oozed ceramic and milk chocolate notes, whereas the palate blew this out the water with a big burst of fruit followed by chocolate, all wrapped in a creamy texture. Lovely.

Then we sampled The Glenrothes Vintage Reserve, 40%, matured in 60% refill sherry casks and 40% first-fill bourbon casks delivering dark fruits on the nose with hints of banana and maple syrup. The palate opened up, much like the Bourbon Cask Reserve, to deliver a creamy whisky laden with lots of spices. Ronnie described it as 'refined elegance' and I could not have agreed more.

After a brief interlude to discuss the merits of heralding the past versus championing the progress made in the generations since, we went in for dram number four, The Glenrothes 2001 Vintage, 12 Years Old, 43%, which gave us a delightfully fruity nose and palate: well rounded, sultanas maybe, with a very thick palate.

We then sampled the 1988 Vintage, which had a lot more zing that I expected, almost fizzy and syrupy, with a much drier palate than I would have thought from the nose, and great depth.

As if this was not enough, we finished with a knockout whisky, namely a super limited release from The Glenrothes distilled in 1966, matured for around forty-five years in a first-fill sherry cask. The notes for this one were brief: 'Just wow'.

Now, one of the most interesting parts of The Glenrothes was breakfast at Rothes House, which is no longer an experience that guests can enjoy since it was very much a Ronnie thing.

As my wife will testify, I'm not really one for doing a lot in the kitchen. My distance from the chef's apron is largely down to Kirsty's excellent cooking, but I do play to my strengths when it comes to the liquid side of things. Wine, whisky, cocktails and tea...I'm your man. Problem is, breakfast at Rothes House also required me to know what I'm doing with food.

Left: Spirit safes collect the precious spirit from the stills.

Below: Lovely examples of copper stills doing their thing.

...we finished with a knockout whisky, namely a super limited release from The Glenrothes distilled in 1966

THE DREAM TEAM COOK BREAKFAST

To explain: it is a tradition that the first night you stay in Rothes House with Ronnie you must cook him and your other hosts breakfast the next morning. The breakfast is then reviewed, written up and scored, before being inserted into the 'Breakfast Book'. A really lovely tradition started by Ronnie and Charles Maclean back in the day, by way of Charles thanking Ronnie for being such a marvellous host.

'He's an utter bastard,' Ronnie said of his own alter ego, who would be judging myself and Christopher's efforts in the kitchen the next morning. 'He's very particular and appreciates things done properly,' he added. 'He will mark you out of five Quaichs based on your efforts.' No pressure, then.

I'm not embarrassed to admit that I was absolutely terrified, I needed to do a good job, and I always play to win. Luckily I had Christopher of Bexsonn.com as my breakfast-creating teammate.

Remember what I said about playing to our strengths? Christopher and I did exactly this. As

My distance from the chef's apron is largely down to Kirsty's excellent cooking, but I do play to my strengths when it comes to the liquid side of things

a dab hand in the kitchen and fan of cooking he handled the food side of things and did a bloody good job, whilst I leveraged my brand-building background to create an immersive and engaging breakfast experience to ensure we scored highly.

The day started early, around 6 a.m. After only a couple of hours sleep I got up and started importing and editing a load of photos and videos I had captured during our walks around the distillery the previous day. This was to form the bedrock of the 'wow' experience we were aiming to deliver.

As with all things motion graphics, it took ages, so I left it exporting as I headed into the garden to cut fresh flowers, which I placed into two of the iconic The Glenrothes bottles Christopher and I had polished off and saved the night before. Christopher hit the kitchen big time, almost octopus-like as he masterfully chopped fruit and got the sausages, eggs, bacon and black pudding on the go with perfect timing.

It was pretty apparent that Ronnie, and presumably Alter Ego, were keen historians. The day before, Ronnie had recounted tales of Scottish and English history, intertwining them with intriguing anecdotes about the evolution of the whisky industry through the years. With this in mind it felt only appropriate to serve an historical cocktail. I set about creating the Churchill Breakfast Cocktail, a drink he allegedly sipped between glasses of champagne through the Second World War: cold brew coffee, a generous double measure of The Glenrothes Manse Reserve, a couple of drops of peach bitters, a teaspoon of maple syrup and a sprinkling of cinnamon.

The cocktail was served at the beginning of breakfast and appeared to go down well,

alongside compliments about Alter Ego's shirt and punctuality. Naturally, I was not up for walking about forty minutes to the local store to pick up a paper, so downloaded the day's Times onto my iPad and, right at the last minute, changed the background on the device to a picture I had taken the day before of the The Glenrothes distillery. Something that Ronnie cooed over.

Christopher plated up the fry-up, and wow did it look and smell great. Once served, I hit play on The Glenrothes brand video I had put together, with the theme from the 2014 Glasgow Commonwealth Games as the backing track, and the experience was complete.

Ronnie loved it, we enjoyed it and got through it working well as a team and ultimately scored 4.25 quaichs out of 5...a pretty high score, especially as it was just two of us where most teams had three or more. You know what they say about too many cooks...

Facing page: Christopher, Ronnie and myself about to tuck into breakfast.

Above: Mmmm old casks of The Glenrothes spirit.

Why I chose this chapter's suggested whisky

After the breakfast-making saga, Ronnie took us shooting in the gorgeous Speyside outdoors for the morning. Once back at Rothes House, he showed us the infamous wine and whisky cellar and quickly noticed that I was taking a few photos of bottles, like I do wherever I go, as you'll see on my Instagram.

He asked why I was taking a photo specifically of The Glenrothes 1985 Vintage. I explained it was my birth year, so I always enjoyed seeing bottles distilled during that year. Without hesitation, he handed me a bottle as a memento of my trip. What a guy.

As soon as I returned home I opened the bottle and raised a dram to Ronnie and The Glenrothes with an appreciative smile.

The nose is beautiful: thick, warming, a sweet Speyside that is underpinned by fresh barley notes, which always transport me back to the distillery and the scenic surroundings where this whisky spent years maturing. The palate retains the freshness of the nose but grows thicker the longer you keep it in your mouth, along with hints of vanilla and dark chocolate. The spirit has a medium finish, which you can savour and enjoy.

I appreciate this gem from 1985 is very hard to obtain, so for this chapter I also recommend The Glenrothes Sherry Cask Reserve from their main range, bottled at 40% and matured in first-fill sherry casks from both Spain and America. This whisky delivers a very leathery nose; pinches of spice, orange and wood notes jump out to greet the heavy sherry influence. The palate delivers more sherry, more spice and wisps of ginger. Gorgeous.

IT'S GREAT DRAMS WHISKY TASTING TIME

Think about the nose and palate…
What notes are you getting? Is it…
Sweet? Sour? Smoky? Spicy?
Summer fruits? Winter fruits?
Oakiness? All of these?
None of these?

Try to decode what your nose and palate
are telling you – everyone's experience
with whisky is personal and can
vary so feel free to explore and
understand your senses…

Your notes

_____   _____
_____   _____
_____   _____
_____   _____
_____   _____

**Remember to tell me how you get on with each whisky from the book on
Twitter, Facebook and Instagram: #GreatDramsOfScotland**

 /GreatDrams   @GreatDrams   greatdramsgreg

THE FUTURE

CHAPTER NINETEEN

KINGSBARNS

Suggested whisky:

Kingsbarns New Make (63.5%)

Interestingly, myself and the founder of Wemyss and Kingsbarns, William Wemyss, celebrated Wemyss Malts' tenth anniversary together. We held a whisky tasting in December 2015 where we kept things relaxed and enjoyed fantastic whiskies from their archives with around twenty or so whisky enthusiasts.

In my best Parkinson impression, I interviewed William to hear him tell the story in his own words of the unique Wemyss Malts, from the first bottle to the opening of the family's own distillery. For me the brand represents a shortcut to consumer understanding through flavour-led naming and it has an impressive approach to limited-edition releases. To be a part of this celebration was an honour.

We covered topics such as the biggest challenges William had faced along the way, his proudest moments, how he saw the market developing over the next few years with a cask shortage predicted, what was next for the brand and, of course, how excited he was about the opening of the Kingsbarns distillery.

A distillery I'd had the pleasure of visiting a few months previously…

For me the brand represents a shortcut to consumer understanding through flavour-led naming and it has an impressive approach to limited-edition releases

NEW, AND THOUGHTFULLY DESIGNED

The first thing you notice when you walk in is the 'new distillery smell'; the varnish from the oak, the spirit in the air and the odd whiff of fresh wood used for shelving around the store. What a treat.

Kingsbarns has only been distilling since January 2015 (well, December 2014, as you'll notice in the distillery video, but due to the delay in getting the necessary paperwork from HMRC they didn't start distilling until one month later), with the first casks filled in March 2015.

As such, there is obviously no whisky to bottle or to try as yet, but as it is owned by the Wemyss (pronounced 'weems') family, anyone visiting the distillery is able to try some of the products released under 'Wemyss Malts', their independent bottling brand. These malts include Peat Chimney, Spice King and The Hive – all evocatively named after their taste profile. There is also the Kingsbarns new make itself at a

Left: A cask stencil.

Above: Fantastic visitor centre sensory experiences.

whopping 63.5% (the same strength the spirit is reduced to before putting it into cask – this strength ensures the best and most flavoursome maturation possible), which they bottled in 20cl bottles as a limited run through 2015.

The distillery itself was the vision of a former golf caddy, Doug Clement, who got the idea after many a year telling folk at the nearby St Andrews golf course that there was no distillery nearby, and then wondering why there wasn't one. After a couple of years planning, he was granted a £640,000 European Food Processing and Marketing grant from the government. He then brought Wemyss on board, who subsequently invested a further £5 million in 2012 to get the distillery built and the whole operation up and running.

The water is drawn from 300-million-year-old sandstone 100 metres beneath the ground, which allows it to maintain a constant temperature. There are no plans to use peated barley from this former farm, and the unpeated barley that's used is grown twenty miles away on a farm owned by the family. This really is a

'barley to bottle' story wrapped up into one tidy parcel of provenance, with 30 tonnes of barley being required per month.

Once spirit has been distilled on the gorgeous stills and run through the central and very shiny spirit safe, it is then poured into casks. Around 60 casks are filled at a time, which are then transferred to a bonded warehouse in central Fife where they will lie maturing until such time as the whisky is bottled, the tax paid and the bottles released from bond in order for us all to enjoy the Kingsbarns whisky in all its glory.

All in all, this is a quaint place that exudes craft whilst simultaneously housing the highest-spec equipment, which clearly had 'future-proofing' in mind when it was all lovingly put together.

Above: Spirit safe.

Right: Mash tun.

Far right: New stills doing their thing.

The visitor centre itself takes guests on both an immersive and a sensory adventure. Props such as old cow horns that contain the various scents you would expect to find within whisky lie waiting to test the nose of each guest. You can also find a restored eighteenth-century 'doocot' there, which holds the first official cask filled at Kingsbarns; this was obviously an exhibit I insisted on sharing a selfie with.

There's also a restaurant for those wishing to enjoy a coffee and a bite.

The small design details that are present the whole way through this distillery really do make it a superb one to visit. From the carved Glencairns in the tasting room and lifts built in for guest accessibility, to the photos of the history of both the family involved and also the site in general, no stone is left unturned.

The small design details that are present the whole way through this distillery really do make it a superb one to visit

Left: My first visit to the distillery.

Below: A display within the visitor centre.

Why I chose this chapter's suggested whisky

The Kingsbarns New Make I speak of will be mainly matured in bourbon casks from the Heaven Hill distillery in America. The exact business plan is still under lock and key (in the spirit safe, I wonder?), with around 140,000 litres of spirit being produced each year on the current production plan, and the capacity to expand to 600,000 litres of spirit at full production.

And it tastes sublime – a fresh, grassy and powerful nose followed by a fruity, warming and slightly citrus palate that is ever so slightly malty. I genuinely cannot wait to taste the matured spirit once it's released in a few years.

CHAPTER TWENTY

KILCHOMAN

Suggested whisky:

Kilchoman Original Cask Strength 2009

Kilchoman was the first new distillery built on Islay for 125 years, and as such required a lot of work when the Wills family started building it in 2004.

The family already had pedigree in the whisky industry: Anthony Wills, Kilchoman's founder, was an independent bottler of whisky for nearly a decade before he set out to create an old-school, honest farm distillery, just like those of yesteryear.

From the very start Wills wanted to own every part of the production, from growing barley, to malting, to distilling, to maturing, to bottling.

And thus the Kilchoman distillery was born on Rockside Farm, not only for its location but also strategically placed to capitalise on Islay's international reputation for both cult and volume single-malt brands. As luck would have it, the Wills had the ideal building setup already in place. According to the family, the farm has the 'best malting barley on the island'.

Things were not plain sailing for the family, however; having started production in December 2005 they experienced a kiln fire in the distillery only three or four months later. Thankfully the fire was contained and did not destroy the whole site. But the ordeal was one to put down to learning curves; now the kiln is using the oil-fired indirect heating which replaced the previous direct heating system. The former system was also apparently quite inefficient in comparison, and after it rebelled by trying to burn the place down, it had to go.

Kilchoman was the first new distillery built on Islay for 125 years...

All has been well since then and over the next few years the Wills expanded their production capacity to 150,000 litres of spirit per year. This is one of the smallest production capacities in Scotland. To put it in context, this annual production is around the same as Caol Ila produces in around a week. Yep. This is truly small batch.

Kilchoman have already created some incredible releases, from their first bottled whisky in 2009 to their now iconic 100% Islay release from 2011. The intent is clear: this is not a family with ambitions to play about in the whisky industry; this is a family with bona fide distilling credentials who have created not only a solid product but a solid brand.

When speaking with Peter Wills, Anthony's son who is fully involved in all things Kilchoman, he told me that the 100% Islay is the bottle that he and the family are most proud of. When I asked why, it was clear that, for Peter, the joy is in discussing the whisky with its drinkers. He recounted how consumers assume that all Scotch whisky is made in this way, but in reality in the entire Scotch whisky industry, as of the beginning of 2016, this is the only distillery to grow, harvest, malt, mash, distil, mature, bottle in one site. Kilchoman's existence thrives on doing something a little different.

This Islay whisky brand's bottle was designed to be premium from the start: heavy glass, embossing, metal 'medals' pressed into the shoulders of the bottle and a bespoke wood-topped cork stopper. All of these are premium cues, all of which are expected from 'heritage' Scotch whisky brands after years of production, not from start-up batch producers like Kilchoman.

The actual filling of the bottles then happened whenever anyone had a free moment to sit at the table. An amazing process when you consider that eight or nine thousand bottles were filled using teapots from the café, before the staff labelled them by hand. This process took just over two months in all, and was the catalyst that made Anthony decide to buy the bottle-filling equipment they have now. I'm guessing the staff are delighted!

...over the next few years the Wills expanded their production capacity to 150,000 litres of spirit per year. This is one of the smallest production capacities in Scotland

Left: True craft distilling at its best.

A LOOK BEHIND THE CURTAIN

Speaking of the bottling hall, or rather 'small room', it's a fascinating place to visit and see its components: bottles, corks, medals, and shrinks to seal the bottles all have their place. This is something you don't really see at large bottling halls, certainly not with such intimacy anyway. All of these components hail from different corners of the globe, before coming together in this small room to be assembled and sealed by hand. The beauty of it is that the bottles are then boxed and shipped back to all of the far-flung places they came from, to be toasted and enjoyed.

More recently, in 2015, the family purchased the farm adjacent to the distillery in order to increase barley growth to an estimated 150 tonnes per annum. The idea is that this extra crop will service the distillery and increase their barley-to-bottle production…significantly.

I've visited the distillery a couple of times and it really runs an interesting operation, from the casks lying around outside ready to be filled, to the floor maltings and the small tasting room which conveniently leads to a café full of locally made cakes, hot food and nice coffee (something that only Kilchoman and Ardbeg offer on Islay, for some reason). This is hands-on craft distilling.

*I've visited the distillery a couple of times and
it really runs an interesting operation*

In the next year or so Kilchoman are planning to build a slightly bigger malt floor and kiln facilities to take production up to around 190,000–200,000 litres per annum over the next few years. Peter Wills told me that this was their defined ceiling for production; they are not interested in going any higher than this, as maintaining their batch and craft status is paramount. It will be interesting to see what the future holds…

When I last spoke to Peter, he regaled stories of how they made plenty of mistakes along the way: the first steam pipes they had were all too small, the bucket conveyor in the malt hall was too small to function properly. They even experimented with countless ways of getting the maltings right – by hand, in wheelbarrows, using a big sheet and dragging, forklift lifting in a bucket, but the malt kept getting crushed so they gave up and stuck to their original setup.

Why I chose this chapter's suggested whisky

Bottled at a powerful 59.2%, this release of Kilchoman Original Cask Strength, which is limited to 9,200 bottles, is a vatting of 35 casks, all ex-bourbon, that were distilled five years ago in 2009. It is a thing of beauty.

Anthony Wills, managing director of Kilchoman, talks about this whisky as: '[my] intention to release a cask strength expression once we had the stock available. This is the way single malt should be drunk. It allows everyone to experience Kilchoman with all the characteristics captured in the glass.' And I could not agree more.

The nose is pretty thick and buttery with bonfire embers and wisps of salty peat. Not as overpowering as the ABV would suggest. The peat gives you a slap around the face once you take a sip thanks to its really dry, chocolatey notes, but is still relatively thick and definitely enjoyable. The finish is not overly long but reiterates the palate and reintroduces the saltiness from the nose. Incidentally, Peter Wills cited this whisky as his favourite, too.

Below: The first Kilchoman tasting I took part in, in the small but impressive visitor centre at the distillery.

CHAPTER TWENTY-ONE

INDEPENDENT BOTTLERS

Suggested whisky:

**Rock Oyster, an SMWS release of your choice,
or a single-cask release from Wemyss**

The importance of independent bottlers for the future of Scotch can be underestimated. Brands are moving to more and more NAS releases, as discussed earlier, and I believe this to be a positive thing for the industry. As a result, independent bottlers such as Douglas Laing, Gordon & Macphail, The Scotch Malt Whisky Society, Wemyss and others will become the sources of some of the most interesting and unique single-cask expressions from both dead and existing distilleries.

In case you are unaware, independent bottlers buy casks from distilleries all over Scotland and the world, and lay them down to mature in their own warehouses (or sometimes at the distilleries where they were distilled, depending on contracts and maturation policy). Bottling happens when they feel the whisky is ready.

My viewpoint is that independent bottlers are a great way to surprise yourself and learn about what each distillery can do.

I'm always curious about the dexterity of a distillery. From an 8 Year Old sherry matured Ardbeg release from SMWS in 2015 (arguably one of the best whiskies I've ever tried) to Rock Oyster, a vatted malt from Douglas Laing, to the 75 Year Old Mortlach from Gordon & Macphail, which defied expectation to be an incredible whisky despite the age, I'm repeatedly impressed.

We would never have experienced these phenomenal liquids had it not been for independent bottlers who sat on a cask for seventy-five years, who thought of vatting several distilleries' wares together to create an amalgamated flavour profile for each region of Scotland, and who also thought to release a young sherry-matured whisky as it was already awesome.

Independent bottlers are bold. They are innovative. They are led by the same curiosity that drives me in what I do within the whisky industry. Now let's look at a few of them in more detail.

DOUGLAS LAING

Aside from being around since the same year as my mother, 1948 (something I'm sure she will hate me stating in print), Douglas Laing has always been proud of its tradition of producing what it describes as 'small batch and artisan bottlings' of Scotch whisky.

My personal favourite is Rock Oyster (more about this below), a vatted malt that aims to capture the flavour profile of the Island region of Scotland in every glass. I think it delivers, and consistently scores highly when used in GreatDrams whisky tastings as a favourite of attendees. Rock Oyster makes up one of five so-called 'Remarkable Regional Malts' alongside The Epicurean, a vatting of lowland malts; Timorous Beastie, a vatting of Highland single malts; Big Peat, a vatting of Islay single malts; and Scallywag, a vatting of Speyside single malts.

Douglas Laing also releases single casks from distilleries, new, old and dead periodically, and all typically do well when reviewed. The thing I love most about the company, however, is how such a small team can not only generate such impressive revenues but also create such a mix of both logic and instinct-driven whisky releases. I was fortunate enough to get some time with Fred Laing, whose father, Fred Douglas Laing, set up the business back in 1948, whilst visiting their offices in Glasgow, and in just that short time I got an incredible insight into the man, the business and the team.

As we sat in his office sipping single cask 54 Year Old North British grain whisky, followed by a single cask 42 Year Old Garnheath, I asked him about the 'birth' of Big Peat. 'Ah... Big Peat,' Fred said with an affectionate smile rising in the right corner of his mouth, 'now that was an interesting one.'

Fred went on to tell me how this expression was created after it became apparent that some people he was working with on other projects were unable to buy a Port Ellen but wanted to try a whisky that typified Islay.

The character himself was the result of a graphic designer live-sketching a stream of consciousness from Fred as he described the scene he saw when sampling this meaty, peaty dram: a happy bearded fisherman fresh from a day at sea in need of a blast of Islay power before heading home for dinner.

The brilliance is that the initial release was supposed to last a year, with a further release pencilled in for twelve months later. The initial run sold out in three months and there has since been a series of limited editions and local versions for different markets; a global persona was born that has engaged whisky drinkers and even inspired tattoos, including one on a very good friend of mine, Tom Thomson who owns TomsWhiskyReviews.com. Incredible.

Douglas Laing is so much more than the Remarkable Regional Malts though. In Provenance, Old Particular and XOP (Xtra Old Particular) you have a series of releases that capture a moment in time for each distillery at which they were distilled. From the 30 Year Old Port Ellen, to the 18 Year Old Springbank, to the 40 Year Old Bunnahabhain, to the 13 Year Old Auchentoshan, I sampled them all with their global malt ambassador Jan Beckers in the same meeting. They all have a story, all stand out for different reasons and all exemplify what it is to be a superb Scotch single malt.

Below: Greg and Fred Laing enjoying a couple of very old whiskies – such a lovely man.

Douglas Laing has always been proud of its tradition of producing what it describes as 'small batch and artisan bottlings' of Scotch whisky

Left: Enjoying a dram at the home of SMWS; The Vaults in Leith.

Below: A load of really old SMWS releases.

THE SCOTCH MALT WHISKY SOCIETY – SMWS

As John McCheyne, brand ambassador for the Society has said to me once or thrice: 'Don't graduate to single cask, start there!'

I've been a member of The Scotch Malt Whisky Society for a few years and have lots of its iconic green bottles in my collection. Its founding principle was to enable the exploration and discovery of new and wonderful whisky. To do this, SMWS de-brand their bottles, leaving numeric references to distilleries and releases so you don't immediately know what distillery you are drinking from, although you do get used to the number system after a while, particularly if you become fond of certain styles.

What sets SMWS apart is that it gives each release a name and lists countless evocative tasting notes that transport you to another place. When I read each name and tasting note before I sip the precious liquid, I always conjure an image in my mind as to what I'm experiencing that's fuelled by the name.

A great example of this is one I bought a couple of as it was so good: SMWS G10.5 A Schweppervescence Moment. The label reads: 'After a clean and citrusy start, turning fruity; ripe kiwis and pineapple cubes. The taste neat of toasted banana bread with butter and plum jam. With water an initial sweet sugar rush then citrusy and sour. Angostura Bitter, Cider and Bitter Lemon.'

At around £130 for your first year's membership, which significantly decreases from your second year, you get access to the organisation's private-member bars globally, as well as access to whiskies for purchase that are limited to only a few hundred at a time as they are single cask, all bottled at cask strength.

SMWS has more than 25,000 members globally, and has been around for more than 30 years. Originally, a bunch of friends got together with a view to experiencing new whiskies and just last year the Society went independent again, having enjoyed a few years ownership by Glenmorangie.

The Society is actually the largest bottler of single cask single malt whisky globally.

As John McCheyne, brand ambassador for the Society has said to me once or thrice: 'Don't graduate to single cask, start there!'

GORDON & MACPHAIL – G&M

Independently owned for more than 120 years, and still family run, the beginnings of this independent bottler is reminiscent of that of blenders we spoke about earlier, such as John Walker. G&M have their very own grocery store in the heart of Elgin, Speyside, which now sells a vast array of whiskies from all over Scotland and beyond.

G&M is all about wood. Its cask and wood management is one of its specialities, that and holding on to casks for an amazing amount of time. In fact the company launched a campaign in 2015 titled 'The Wood Makes the Whisky', which communicated the differences in cask type and maturation duration, showing how time and wood are interlinked. In G&M's eyes, this relationship between timber and time is all part of the quest to create the highest quality whisky.

In 2015 G&M released the oldest commercially bottled whisky in the world: Mortlach 75 Years Old, matured in a first-fill sherry butt cask with only 100 bottles as part of their Generations range. I was lucky enough to be a part of the launch.

Primarily, G&M release expressions under its independent bottling ranges: Cask Strength, Connoisseurs Choice, Private Collection, Distillery Labels, Generations, Rare Old, Rare Vintage and others.

Gordon & Macphail also owns the Benromach distillery in Speyside, a distillery with the mantra of 'time-honoured and traditional' sitting at the heart of every drop of whisky it distils and matures. Having said that, the packaging has a more light-hearted and naïve feel, iconified in its teardrop graphic symbol and youthful font that's more contemporary than generational.

The whisky itself feels of a somewhat old-school nature, like the Speyside whiskies of the 1960s: light smoke with a balanced mouth feel and palate that is surprisingly quaffable.

All in all, I think they have created a great range in Benromach, surprising in places, with my favourites being the Peat Smoke and 100% Proof. If you forced my hand, Peat Smoke just about edges it. I still cannot quite get on board with that font though, but if that's the only fault I can find in a range that will satisfy a wide variety of whisky drinkers, I can live with it.

In 2015 G&M released the oldest commercially bottled whisky in the world: Mortlach 75 Years Old

Left: Greg and Charles Maclean.

Right: The chosen dram for this chapter.

Below: Fabulous releases from Wemyss Malta.

WEMYSS

Wemyss (pronounced 'weems') was founded by William Wemyss (see chapter 19, page 174) in 2005 after a long involvement with the Scotch whisky industry, which included growing crops for producers including John Haig. In the end, it made sense to start releasing blended malt whisky independently under his own brand.

Similar to SMWS, Wemyss often gives its bottles intriguing names. One of its first bottles, and my favourite, although sadly unavailable nowadays, is called Smooth Gentleman. It's a general rule that the name of the whisky for Wemyss (in this case 'smooth') is determined by its flavour and aroma, giving shoppers a helpful aid when navigating the range. Their current line-up includes The Hive, Spice King and Peat Chimney.

Wemyss embodies everything consumers should associate with a craft spirits operation. The organisation is mostly centred on the export market, shipping not hundreds of thousands or millions of cases of whisky, but thousands of cases. These volumes are small enough to keep the brand nimble when it comes to consumer needs and market availability of whisky, but large enough to be relevant to a critical mass of whisky drinkers.

Wemyss' interesting single-cask releases lead to renewed focus on its brand name and portfolio for PR and social media exposure. The overarching message for its single-cask range seems to be that 'when its gone its gone'; this is a premium and exclusive range of the brand's, but fear not, its blended malt whisky range is going nowhere in a hurry.

Wemyss embodies everything consumers should associate with a craft spirits operation

Why I chose this chapter's suggested whisky

Rock Oyster was one of my favourite whiskies of the year for 2015 for its punchy yet discerning nose and palate, and it is sensibly priced. I share it often in whisky tastings and it always goes down well, mostly with a nodding agreement that this is a great whisky for an almost-too-good-to-be-true price.

A vatted malt that oozes salty maritime notes coupled with toffee and just the right amount of smoke, it comprises whiskies from distilleries on islands such as Jura, Arran, Orkney and Islay. Intense, with just the right amount of punch and sweetness, this is just great. Go buy a bottle, now. That's an order.

If that does not float your boat, pick up any SMWS release and explore something special; try one of the bottles starting with 'G' to see what a grain whisky is like. Another option would be to check out the latest single-cask releases from Wemyss as they are constantly discovering gems.

IT'S GREAT DRAMS WHISKY TASTING TIME

Think about the nose and palate…
What notes are you getting? Is it…
Sweet? Sour? Smoky? Spicy?
Summer fruits? Winter fruits?
Oakiness? All of these?
None of these?

Try to decode what your nose and palate
are telling you – everyone's experience
with whisky is personal and can
vary so feel free to explore and
understand your senses…

Your notes

_____   _____
_____   _____
_____   _____
_____   _____
_____

**Remember to tell me how you get on with each whisky from the book on
Twitter, Facebook and Instagram:** #GreatDramsOfScotland

 /GreatDrams   @GreatDrams   greatdramsgreg

CHAPTER TWENTY-TWO

FINAL THOUGHTS

Suggested whisky:

**Your favourite from all we have been
through on this journey together**

I hope you enjoyed The GreatDrams of Scotland. From what started off as a Post-it note on the wall in my office to where we are today, it has been illuminating and fascinating to put together. I've been impressed and am so grateful for the time people have taken out to talk to me. Some of you are listed on page 208, but know that all of you are the reason I love working in this industry so much.

In case you're interested, I always like to keep notes and statistics of my journey through various projects, so here are a few of my favourites relating to this book:

- June 2015 – Idea committed to paper
- August 2015 – When the book was started in SMWS, 19 Greville Street, London (my favourite place to get the creative juices flowing)
- 21 – The amount of flights I have used to research and/or write elements of the book
- 104 – The original number of brands I wanted to include; a tad ambitious
- 23 – The number of brands I ended up including
- 15 – The number of cities in which I have spent time whilst working on the book
- 6 – The number of Apple devices this book has been typed on
- 2 – The number of Windows devices this book has been proofread on
- Countless – The amount of selfies at distilleries you'll find on my Instagram

*To adapt a line from one of my favourite movie series, James Bond:
GreatDrams will return for more in this series*

THE GREAT DRAMS SPECIALIST WHISKY RETAILERS LIST

There are so many specialist retail stores for whisky drinkers nowadays; no matter what you are looking for there is likely a retailer who has it or at least can get it. Here I've included a list of my favourites to help you navigate the world of options available to you.

Abbey Whisky
www.abbeywhisky.com
Beautiful website with a great range of unique and desirable whiskies – you can get lost looking around it for ages, or at least I can…

Cadenheads
www.whiskytastingroom.com
Well priced, all about the whisky; Cadenhead's have tons of impressive casks in their warehouses that they then bottle independently and release at a fair cost. They also own the Springbank and Glengyle distilleries so stock numerous expressions that you'll love. Regular out-turns full of expressions you'd otherwise not be able to try.

Douglas Laing
www.douglaslaing.com
One of my favourites, they have regular out-turns of new independently bottled Scotch whiskies with options to suit every budget and every flavour profile.

Green Welly Shop
www.thegreenwellystop.co.uk/whiskyshop
'Whisky Galore at The Green Welly Stop – Selling Scotch Whisky since 1976'. A useful place for limited editions and hard to find whiskies, they get all kinds of expressions in, some of the best availability in the business.

Hard to Find Whiskies
www.htfw.com
The name says it all really; specialists in stocking hard to find whiskies, they have some ridiculously desirable bottles in stock and get new bottles in regularly so make sure to check back often to see what else you can add to your collection.

Master of Malt
www.masterofmalt.com
This is a fantastic site to go to if you want a little bit more detail on your purchase than with other sites. Master of Malt gives a run-down of key details for every whisky as well as tasting notes for most expressions.

Royal Mile Whiskies
www.royalmilewhiskies.com
Royal Mile Whiskies, and the great people behind it, have hundreds of superb whiskies. Easy to navigate online and awesome to spend time in their stores looking, let alone buying!

The Whisky Shop Dufftown
www.whiskyshopdufftown.com
The focus is on whisky, great bottles and the store is a treasure trove of whisky gems and the site carries some lovely bottles both mainstream and rare.

The Whisky Shop

www.whiskyshop.com

At The Whisky Shop there are three defined zones: 'Show me', 'Tell me' and 'Sell me' that help buyers navigate the store whether they are a whisky connoisseur or they are a first time whisky buyer. As you enter the store you will notice that there is a lot of light, framing each bottle both individually and as a collective to show off the different brands and the regions the whiskies hail from.

The Whisky Exchange

www.thewhiskyexchange.com

They have just about every whisky from around the world that you could imagine. The Whisky Exchange has an easy to navigate website that is great for finding exactly what you want, or just browsing when you're in the mood for something new.

INDEX

THANK YOUS

As cheesy as it is to say, this book could not have been possible without the help of some incredible people in my life and in the whisky industry. In no particular order, I would like to thank:

Kirsty Dillon: my wife, for all her love, support, encouragement and belief in what I do. You get my drive and my passions and embrace them. I will always be thankful.

Ann Dillon: my mum, aww, for believing and for referring to my blog as an 'online diary', which prompted a 30-minute explanation, using Post-Its, a white board and diagrams, as to how GreatDrams works as a business.

Megan Brownrigg: GreatDrams assistant who has proofed this book (so all typos and elongated sentences that still remain are her fault) and has been incredibly helpful.

Rebecca Dillon: GreatDrams assistant who has helped with the research and content side of GreatDrams for a while now and makes my life easier!

Natasha Najm: my publicist who not only has an incredible passion for whisky and this fabulous industry and has helped so much with getting this book out there, but has also challenged me to do things differently.

Bailey and Malibu: my pensioner cats who, without knowing, had virtually all of this book narrated to them multiple times as I played with sentence structure and content themes. Bailey especially, your warmth during the winter writing months was much appreciated.

The #whiskyfabric: you guys have all been so welcoming, encouraging, banterous and insightful, inspirational, you are all awesome and I enjoy dramming with you all, including, in alphabetical order: Billy Abbott, Kevin Abrook, Shilton Almeida, Iain Allen, Jan Beckers, Ivan Bell, Anne-Sophie Bigot, Chris Borrow, Blair Bowman, Dave Broom, James Brown, Ian Buxton, Matt Chambers, Ben Cops, Ronnie Cox, Jonathan Driver, Kara Duggan, Colin Dunn, Martin Eber, Yoav Gelbfish, Alwynne Gwilt, Tim Hain, Daryl Haldane, Colin Hampden-White, Joel Harrison, Emma Hooper, Ian Hunter, Jill Inglis, Mark Jennings, Serena Kaye, Cara Laing, Fred Laing, Amanda Ludlow, Eddie Ludlow, Mr. Lyan, Neil Macdonald, Sam Macdonald, Charles Maclean, John McCheyne, Jonny McMillan, Eddie Nara, Mark Newton, Nathan Nye, Becky Paskin, James Porteous, Steve Prentice, Kat Priestly, Andrew Purslow, Neil Ridley, Jenny Rogerson, Steve Rush, Kristiane Sherry, Ian Taylor, Karen Taylor, Mark Thomson, Tom Thomson, Herman van Broekhuizen, Matt Veira, Jon Webb, William Wemyss, Chris 'Tiger' White, Dave Worthington, Nicola Young, and many more.